QUICK & EASY
Cross Stitch Gifts

Oxmoor House®

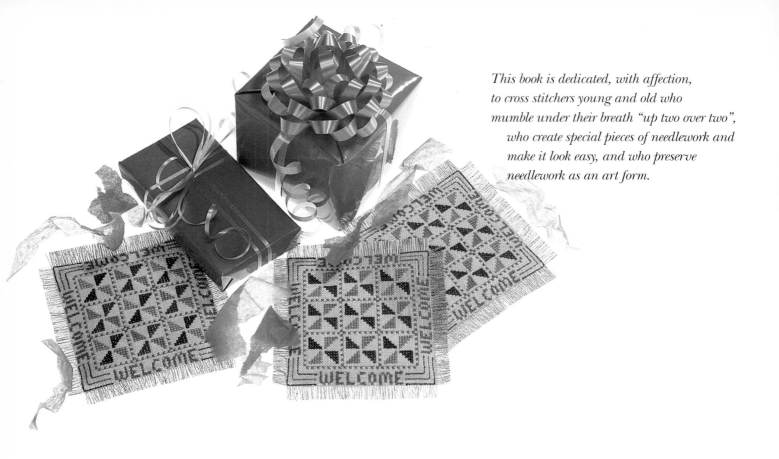

*This book is dedicated, with affection,
to cross stitchers young and old who
mumble under their breath "up two over two",
who create special pieces of needlework and
make it look easy, and who preserve
needlework as an art form.*

Quick & Easy Cross Stitch Gifts
from *The Joys of Cross Stitch* series

©1991 by Oxmoor House, Inc.
Book Division of Southern Progress Corporation
P.O. Box 2463
Birmingham, Alabama 35201

Library of Congress Catalog Card Number: 90-64131
ISBN: 0-8487-1069-X
ISSN: 0890-8222
Manufactured in the United States of America
First Printing 1991

Executive Editor: Nancy J. Fitzpatrick
Director of Manufacturing: Jerry Higdon
Associate Production Manager: Rick Litton
Production Assistant: Theresa L. Beste

Symbol of Excellence Publishers, Inc. Staff

Editors: Barbara Cockerham, Phyllis Hoffman
Associate Editor: Diane Kennedy
Production Vice President: Wayne Hoffman
Creative Director: Mac Jamieson
Art Director: Yukie McLean
Associate Production Manager: Perry James
Editorial Assistants: Donna Rush, Carol Odom
Senior Computer Graphics Designer: Scott Begley
Computer Graphics Designers: Janet Roberts, Keith Lawler
Assistant Art Director: Casey Day
Photography Stylist: Tracey MacMillan
Studio Assistant: Clay Wortham
Designers: Cathy Livingston, Keith Lawler, Linda Jary,
    Robyn Taylor, Dot Young, Teresa Wentzler, Pat Phillips
Stitchers: Lorna Ables, Katherine Bousack, Nora Bowen,
    Vanessa Bragg, Denise Brown, Jalyn Burns,
    Bettye Dwyer, Theresa Ewing, Melissa Gachet,
    Patsy Gilley, Shelia Gray, Tamela Gregg, Steve Haygood,
    Mary Lou Hilton, Cindy Hollingsworth, Elane Jones,
    Joan Lanier, Linda Mantonya, Theresa May,
    Felicia McEachin, Kara Miller, Rebecca Mitchell,
    Catherine Scott, Karen Taylor, Debbie Templeton,
    Andrea Tyus, Tammy Webber, Debra Woolridge

Contents

Introduction

Cross stitch is perfection—plain and simple perfection—neat little stitches placed side by side on evenly woven fabric. Cross stitch lets us be creative in any way we choose, be it a country welcome or a traditional Christmas sampler. Cross stitch lets us tell of ourselves—who we are and our likes and preferences—by the stitchery we have completed, for ourselves or for family and friends.

We know of no other hobby which can so effectively serve to relieve the stress of busy days, which is so quickly addictive, and which results in such wonderful, heart-warming gifts.

Selecting this collection of cross stitch designs, which are especially suited for stitching and giving as gifts, has been fun for us. As we evaluated each design, we visualized it as a token of love from the hands of a stitcher. We knew the designs had to fit our criteria of quick and easy. Many of the designs are surprisingly quick to stitch, and yet they make charming gifts. Others take longer to complete, but are keepsakes well worth the extra time. We think you'll find, in these five chapters, gift ideas for every occasion.

Giving cross stitched gifts brings us pleasure in many ways. First there is the satisfaction of knowing we have selected just the right design to stitch as a gift for a particular person. Then there is the very real pleasure of spending our time creating the piece. Seeing the delight shining in the gift recipient's face is yet another reward

4

for our efforts. After stitching cross stitched gifts for 18 years, we have discovered that, when we select a design with someone in mind, and think of that person as we stitch the piece, the completed piece is truly theirs. To keep it for ourselves, or to give it to another person, would be unthinkable.

From towel borders and box toppers to a reminder board for college students, from Halloween treat bags to Christmas samplers, from baby accessories to graduation kudos, all these designs and many more suited for special occasions are found in these pages. So pull your needlework basket close by your stitching chair, select a favorite, and enjoy stitching!

Gifts For The Home

Make gift-giving occasions memorable with a present you have stitched for the lucky recipient's home.

Four Seasons

Four Seasons, a summer-bright display of seasonal stitchery, will add pizzazz to any home and make you the hero of any occasion. Familiar fruits and berries representing the four seasons grace a variety of gifts, from a quilted wall hanging to a versatile table runner. Five of the smaller motifs have been stitched for use as jar toppers on gifts of preserved jams, jellies, and relishes. Pick your favorite fruit design and stitch a bread cover for a quick-to-complete gift. We've used a pre-finished place mat and napkin as a table runner and a bread cover.

SPRING

	DMC	COLOR
c	842	beige-brown, very light
L	327	antique violet, dark
3	743	yellow, medium
z	3347	yellow-green, medium
⁄	3346	hunter green
x	309	rose, deep
o	720	orange spice, dark
=	801	coffee brown, dark

Fabric used for model: 28-count tan Jobelan from Wichelt Imports, Inc.

Stitch count: 106H x 106W
Approximate design size:
14-count—7 ½" x 7 ½"
18-count—5 ⅞" x 5 ⅞"
28-count—7 ⅝" x 7 ⅝"

Instructions: Cross stitch over two threads using three strands of floss. Turn to pages 12 and 140 for finishing instructions.
Note: Fabric used for jar lids—14-count white Aida; Place mat and napkin (used as table runner and bread cover)—14-count country oatmeal Royal Classics from Charles Craft, Inc.

SUMMER

Fabric used for model: 28-count tan Jobelan from Wichelt Imports, Inc.

Stitch count: 106H x 106W

	DMC	COLOR
C	842	beige-brown, very light
Z	3347	yellow-green, medium
X	309	rose, deep
●	3371	black-brown
V	922	copper, light
=	801	coffee brown, dark
L	930	antique blue, dark
╱	743	yellow, medium

Approximate design size:

14-count—7 ½" x 7 ½"

18-count—5 ⅞" x 5 ⅞"

28-count—7 ⅝" x 7 ⅝"

Instructions: Cross stitch over two threads using three strands of floss.

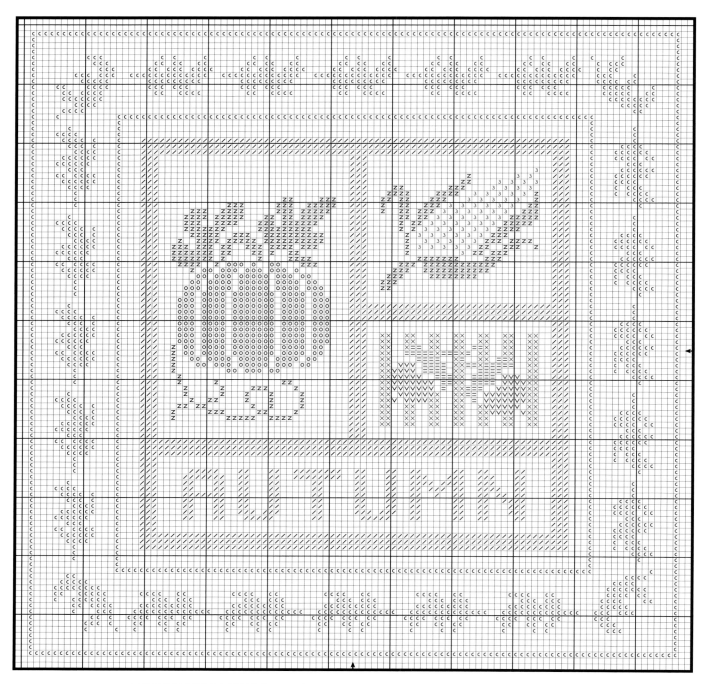

AUTUMN

	DMC	COLOR
c	842	beige-brown, very light
o	720	orange spice, dark
z	3347	yellow-green, medium
╱	920	copper, medium
V	922	copper, light
=	801	coffee brown, dark
x	309	rose, deep
3	743	yellow, medium

Fabric used for model: 28-count tan Jobelan
from Wichelt Imports, Inc.
Stitch count: 106H x 106W
Approximate design size:
14-count—7 ½" x 7 ½"
18-count—5 ⅞" x 5 ⅞"
28-count—7 ⅝" x 7 ⅝"

Instructions: Cross stitch over two threads
using three strands of floss.

WINTER

	DMC	COLOR
c	842	beige-brown, very light
z	3347	yellow-green, medium
3	743	yellow, medium
x	309	rose, deep
⁄	930	antique blue, dark
L	327	antique violet, dark
T	932	antique blue, light
=	801	coffee brown, dark

Fabric used for model: 28-count tan Jobelan
from Wichelt Imports, Inc.
Stitch count: 106H x 106W
Approximate design size:
    14-count—7 ½" x 7 ½"
    18-count—5 ⅞" x 5 ⅞"
    28-count—7 ⅝" x 7 ⅝"

Instructions: Cross stitch over two threads
using three strands of floss.

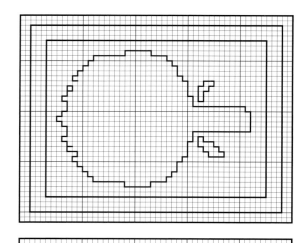

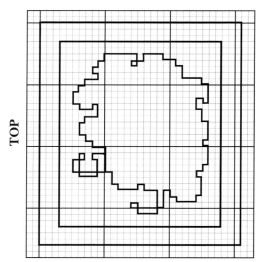

Outlines of fruit for placement on napkin and place mat (used as bread cover and table runner).

QUILTED WALL HANGING INSTRUCTIONS

1. Choose a fabric which complements the design, as well as the room where the finished piece will hang.
2. Cut three fabric strips 7" x 6 ½" to use for hanging tabs.
3. Cut three strips 4" x 25 ½" for horizontal strips.
4. Cut six strips 4" x 8 ½" for vertical strips.
5. Fold hanging tabs in half vertically with right sides together. Using a ½" seam allowance, sew hanging tabs, right sides together. Turn and press.
6. Piece front of wall hanging according to illustration, allowing ⅜" of cross stitch fabric between seam and edge of stitched border.
7. Cut backing 25" x 25".
8. Fold tabs in half and place so they line up with vertical strips (see illustration), and sew in place.
9. Place backing fabric and pieced front right sides together and sew along top edge.
10. Turn right sides out. Insert batting which has been cut to fit top between front and back fabric.
11. Quilt around cross stitched blocks, approximately ¼" from seam.
12. Fold quilt top fabric to back and whipstitch in place.

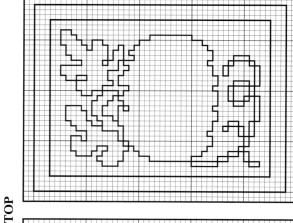

TOP

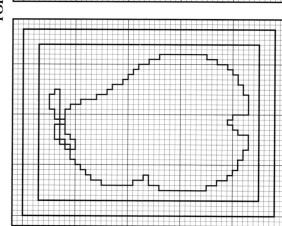

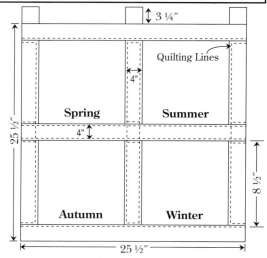

All measurements were made prior to finishing.

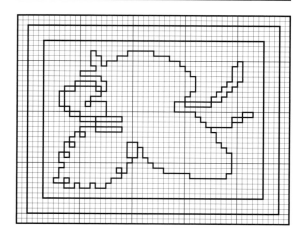

Vegetable Squares

Your gift will make a big impact when you present these light, bright designs called *Vegetable Squares*. Charted with the look of Italian or French tiles, these quickly stitched pieces bring the bounty of the garden to kitchen decor. Combined with familiar kitchen trappings and copper pots, the look is fabulous.

ASPARAGUS

	DMC	COLOR
V	472	avocado, ultra light
o	471	avocado, very light
z	470	avocado, light
II	775	baby blue, light (half cross)
3	775	baby blue, light
N	760	salmon
∴	3328	salmon, medium
x	3042	antique violet, light
bs	610	drab brown, very dark

Fabric used for models: 14-count white Aida
Stitch count: 72H x 72W
Approximate design size:
   14-count—5 ¼" x 5 ¼"
   18-count—4" x 4"

Instructions: Cross stitch using three strands of floss. Backstitch (bs) using two strands 610.

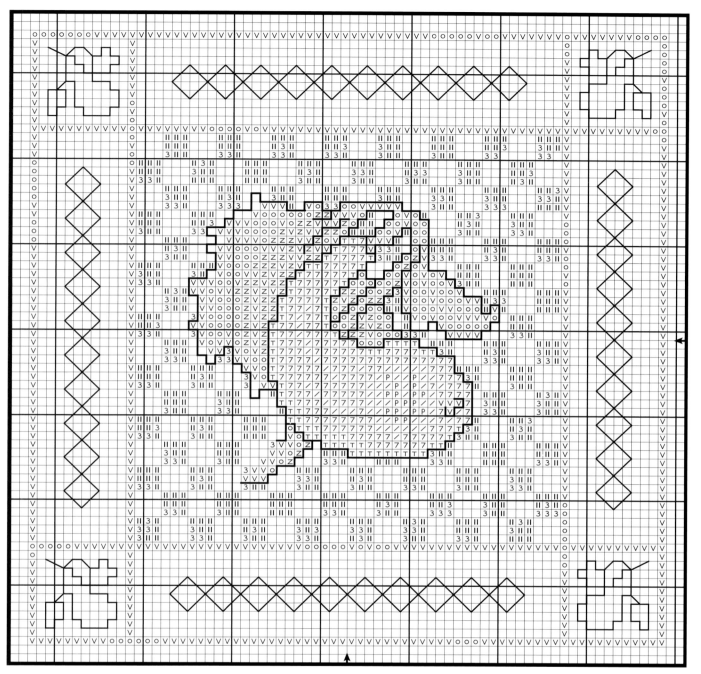

SQUASH

	DMC	COLOR
V	472	avocado, ultra light
o	471	avocado, very light
z	470	avocado, light
‖	775	baby blue, light (half cross)
3	775	baby blue, light
T	725	topaz
7	726	topaz, light
∕	727	topaz, very light
P	white	white
bs	610	drab brown, very dark

Fabric used for models: 14-count white Aida
Stitch count: 72H x 72W
Approximate design size:
    14-count—5 ¼" x 5 ¼"
    18-count—4" x 4"

Instructions: Cross stitch using three strands of floss. Backstitch (bs) using two strands 610.

BEET

	DMC	COLOR
●	603	cranberry
L	602	cranberry, medium
c	601	cranberry, dark
V	472	avocado, ultra light
o	471	avocado, very light
z	470	avocado, light
‖	775	baby blue, light (half cross)
3	775	baby blue, light
bs	610	drab brown, very dark

Fabric used for models: 14-count white Aida
Stitch count: 72H x 72W
Approximate design size:
    14-count—5 ¼" x 5 ¼"
    18-count—4" x 4"

Instructions: Cross stitch using three strands of floss. Backstitch (bs) using two strands 610.

Flower Basket

Send a close friend a touch of spring when you stitch these delicate blooms for her. Two color codes are included, allowing you to create distinctly different pieces from the same design. Embellish hand towels, pillowcases, sachet bags, and a variety of gift items with this versatile flower basket.

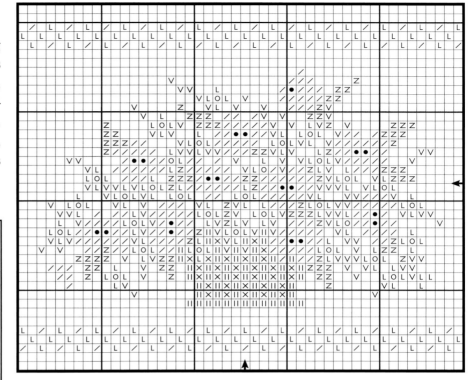

FLOWER BASKET

White

	DMC	COLOR
╱	3326	rose, light
●	309	rose, deep
o	746	off white
L	813	blue, light
V	704	chartreuse, bright
z	701	Christmas green, light
‖	676	old gold, light
x	680	old gold, dark

Buttered Almond

	DMC	COLOR
╱	498	Christmas red, dark
●	902	garnet, very dark
o	729	old gold, medium
L	312	navy blue, light
V	3348	yellow-green, light
z	3346	hunter green
‖	839	beige-brown, dark
x	938	coffee brown, ultra dark

Fabric used for models: 14-count white KitchenMates towel, and 14-count buttered almond KitchenMates towel from Charles Craft, Inc.

Stitch count: 37H x width of towel
Approximate design size:
14-count—2 ⅝" x width of towel

Instructions: Cross stitch using three strands of floss. Stitch border to ends of towel.

Greetings!

Coffee breaks are the best time for a short stitching break. This simple greeting is easily accomplished and can be finished in a variety of interesting ways. The ruffled hoop surrounding the two-color variation is made by gluing pre-gathered eyelet trim to an inexpensive wooden embroidery hoop. Simply pop your completed work into the hoop, tape the excess fabric to the back, and your gift is ready to wrap!

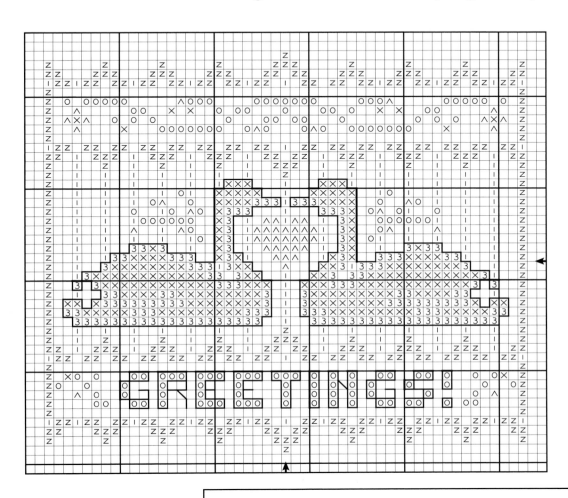

GREETINGS!

	DMC	COLOR
∧	223	pink, medium
I	371	mustard
3	738	tan, very light
z	801	coffee, dark
o	3345	hunter, dark
x	ecru	ecru

Fabric used for model: 14-count ivory Aida
Stitch count: 44H x 51W

Approximate design size:
14-count—3 ¼" x 3 ¾"
18-count—2 ½" x 2 ⅞"

Instructions: Cross stitch using two strands of floss. Backstitch using one strand 3345. Option: This design can also be stitched using two colors. We chose 666 for the heart and 930 for remainder of stitching. Turn to page 141 for finishing instructions.

Welcome To Our Home

Linen fabric, new to many stitchers, provides a more formal background for cross stitch than Aida. The quaint cottage, complete with terra cotta thatch roof, is the focal point of this small welcome. Try your hand at linen and create this lovely display piece for your home. What a wonderful hostess gift this will make!

WELCOME TO OUR HOME

	DMC	COLOR
■	327	antique violet, dark
z	355	terra cotta, dark
ε	356	terra cotta, medium
c	502	blue green
●	677	old gold, very light
x	712	cream
╱	948	peach flesh, very light
V	842	beige-brown, very light
N	3041	antique violet, medium
o	758	terra cotta, light
bs	3371	black-brown
bs	500	blue green, very dark
bs	840	beige-brown, medium
bs	938	coffee brown, ultra dark

Fabric used for model: 27-count natural brown linen from Norden Crafts
Stitch count: 90H x 60W
Approximate design size:
   14-count—6 ½" x 4 ½"
   18-count—5" x 3 ½"
   27-count—6 ⅝" x 4 ⅜"

Instructions: Cross stitch over two threads using two strands of floss. Backstitch using one strand of floss unless otherwise indicated.
Backstitch (bs) instructions:

500	stems (two strands)
840	steps
938	house
3371	fence
356	windows
712	lettering (two strands)

Autumn Welcome

Playful squirrels jumping and gathering acorns for the winter are a favorite sight when the green leaves of summer give way to autumn's glory. In addition to making an attractive welcome for your home, this adorable pair of squirrels can be stitched on a blouse pocket, using waste canvas, to wear with your favorite fall skirt. The border of leaves will work well on the bands of hand towels suited to the season.

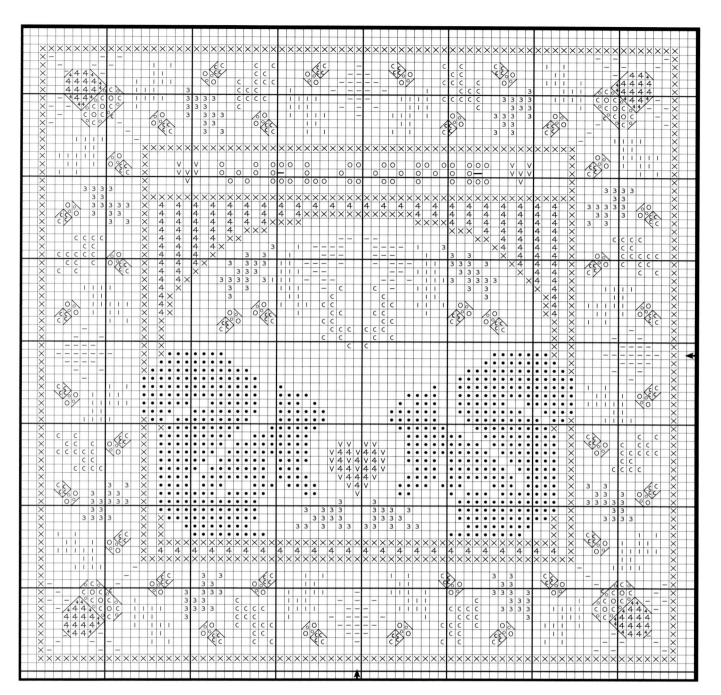

AUTUMN WELCOME

DMC		COLOR
V	919	red-copper
I	780	topaz, very dark
o	829	olive green, very dark
x	610	drab brown, very dark
3	3011	khaki green, dark
4	422	hazelnut brown, light
c	3045	yellow-beige, dark
•	611	drab brown, dark
—	731	olive green, dark

Fabric used for model: 25-count Floba® from Zweigart®

Stitch count: 75H x 75W

Approximate design size:
14-count—5 ⅜" x 5 ⅜"
18-count—4 ¼" x 4 ¼"
25-count—6" x 6"

Instructions: Cross stitch over two threads using three strands of floss. Backstitch (—) in middle of *E*'s in *Welcome* using three strands 829.

Give Thanks

Today's needlewoman uses her skills with the needle and thread to create lasting reminders of important things in her life. In this stitchery of a reassuring verse, the inclusion of the date may add to its meaning in years to come.

GIVE THANKS

	DMC	COLOR
z	319	pistachio green, very dark
V	367	pistachio green, dark
■	347	salmon, dark
x	3328	salmon, medium
3	676	old gold, light

Fabric used for model: 25-count cream Dublin linen from Zweigart®

Stitch count: 81H x 145W
Approximate design size:
    14-count—5 ¾" x 10 ½"
    18-count—4 ½" x 8 ¼"
    25-count—6" x 10 ¾"

Instructions: Cross stitch over two threads using two strands of floss. Backstitch hearts using two strands 347.

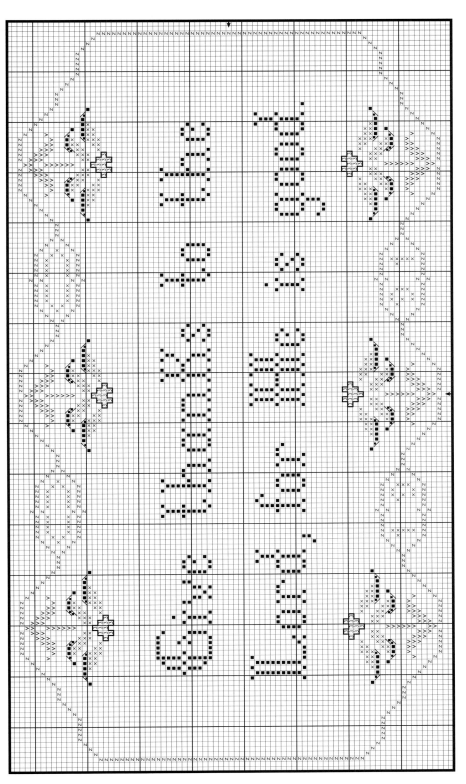

My Quilt And I

A sentiment from a 1905 card served as inspiration for this beautiful piece, which honors the quilt. Quilting, the only true needleart form native to this country, is practiced by avid quilters with the same vigor shown by many cross stitchers of today. If you need a gift for a quilter or a collector of quilts, use this design, and if you wish, make color changes to suit her fancy.

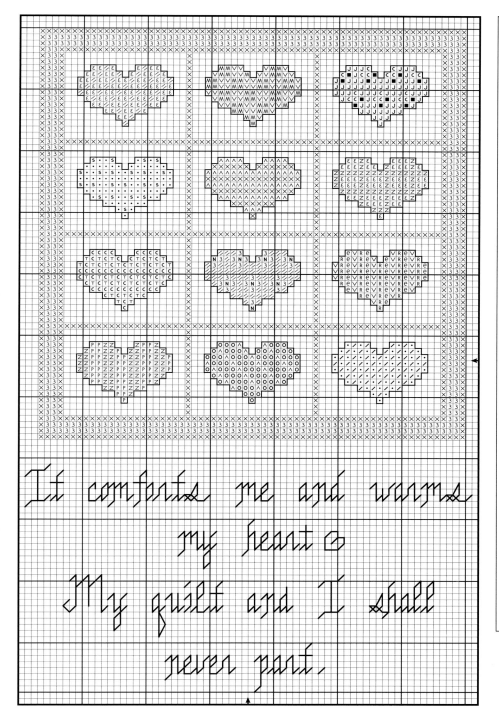

	DMC	COLOR
e	ecru	ecru
N	221	shell pink, dark
3	224	shell pink, light
o	316	antique mauve, medium
s	327	antique violet, dark
T	347	salmon, dark
M	356	terra cotta, medium
■	502	blue green
J	504	blue green, light
•	677	old gold, very light
∕	758	terra cotta, light
c	761	salmon, light
ε	778	antique mauve, light
∕∕	927	gray-green, medium
x	931	antique blue, medium
∧	932	antique blue, light
R	840	beige-brown, medium
V	842	beige-brown, very light
P	3041	antique violet, medium
z	3042	antique violet, light
bs	640	beige-gray, very dark

Fabric used for model: 27-count cream linen from Norden Crafts
Stitch count: 108H x 70W
Approximate design size:
    14-count—7 ¾" x 5"
    18-count—6" x 4"
    27-count—8" x 5 ¼"

Instructions: Cross stitch over two threads using two strands of floss. Backstitch using two strands of floss.
Backstitch (bs) instructions:
    640   hearts
    931   lettering

Gifts
Because I Care

Stitchers who lovingly labor over creative gifts do so because they care deeply about the person who receives their stitchery, and because they are filled with a sense of pride in presenting gifts which reflect their love. Use the charts in this chapter to show you care.

Don't Forget

Know someone who needs a gentle reminder about homework or car-pool day, or a nudge to call home? Choose an insert design to stitch for display in your kitchen or in a young child's room, or to send off to school with your college-bound child. This makes a useful dorm decoration and serves as a constant reminder that you care. Stitch them, present them, then relax and let this clever bulletin board do the rest!

DON'T FORGET (CHILD)

	DMC	COLOR
x	776	pink, medium
⁄	818	baby pink
•	746	off white
<	white	white
o	209	lavender, dark
z	743	yellow, medium
c	905	parrot green, dark
+	335	rose
■	413	pewter gray, dark

Fabric used for model: 25-count cream
Lugana® from Zweigart®
Stitch count: 95H x 50W
Approximate design size:
    14-count—6 ¾" x 3 ½"
    18-count—5 ¼" x 2 ¾"
    25-count—7 ⅝" x 4"

Instructions: Cross stitch over two threads using two strands of floss. Backstitch using two strands of floss unless indicated otherwise. Straight stitch whiskers using one strand 413. Make French knots for periods and dot over *i* using two strands 413, wrapping floss around needle twice. Chart on page 33 may be used to personalize design.
Backstitch (bs) instructions:
    335   name, *Don't Forget* and
           Love, Mom
    413   rabbit and paws (one
           strand), remainder of
           backstitching

DON'T FORGET (KITCHEN)

	DMC	COLOR
■	931	antique blue, medium
∧	932	antique blue, light
2	304	Christmas red, medium
−	498	Christmas red, dark
x	414	steel gray, dark
c	318	steel gray, light
\	415	pearl gray
/	434	brown
>	435	brown, very light
•	987	forest green, dark
<	760	salmon
N	761	salmon, light
o	552	violet, dark
X	553	violet, medium
z	3328	salmon, medium
bs	422	hazelnut brown, light
bs	3371	black-brown

Fabric used for model: 14-count cream Aida
Stitch count: 98H x 51W
Approximate design size:
    14-count—7" x 3 ⅝"
    18-count—5 ½" x 2 ⅞"

Instructions: Cross stitch using two strands of floss. Backstitch using one strand of floss. Make French knots for dots on *i*'s and pressure cooker dial (symbol ⊙) using one strand 3371 wrapping around needle twice.
Backstitch (bs) instructions:
∿∿ 422   ribbon around jar lid
    931   *Don't Forget*
    3371   remainder of backstitching

DON'T FORGET (COLLEGE)

	DMC	COLOR
c	738	tan, very light
x	725	topaz
╱	726	topaz, light
z	321	Christmas red
─	792	cornflower blue, dark
•	676	old gold, light
>	760	salmon
╲	761	salmon, light
■	3371	black-brown

Fabric used for model: 14-count antique white Aida from Charles Craft, Inc.
Stitch count: 98H x 50W
Approximate design size:
14-count—7" x 3 ⅝"
18-count—5 ½" x 2 ¾"

Instructions: Cross stitch using two strands of floss. Backstitch using one strand of floss unless indicated otherwise. Make French knots for dots over *i*'s and colon in *8:00* using one strand 792 wrapping floss around needle twice.
Backstitch (bs) instructions:
3371 *Don't Forget*, pencil
321 vertical line on notebook paper
794 remainder of notebook paper
∿792 list on notebook paper (two strands)

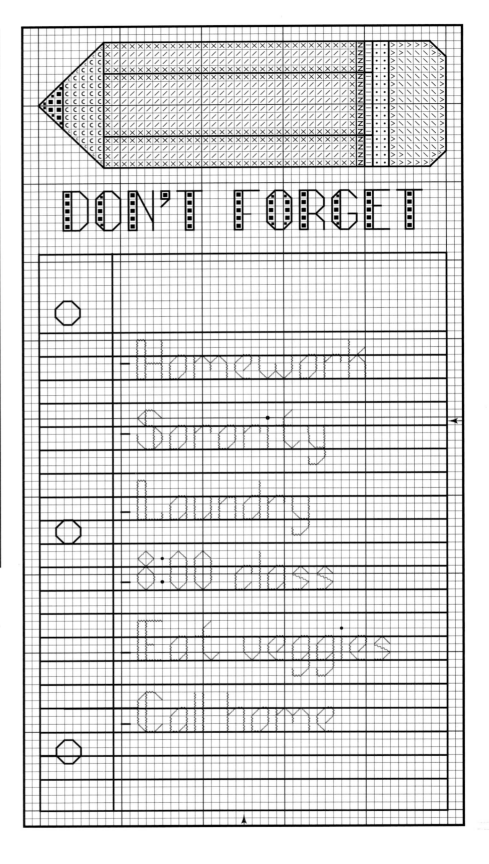

33

Spring Blossom Trio

Everyone enjoys having small accessories to place in out-of-the-way nooks. Decorator easels, commonly available, offer a tabletop display alternative to the traditional hanging of needlework pieces. These floral designs are equally appealing framed tightly without a mat. With the resurgence of floral fabrics used by today's decorators, small floral cross stitched pieces find their home in most any surrounding. The Aida fabric used as ground cloth makes stitching easy, and the results delightful.

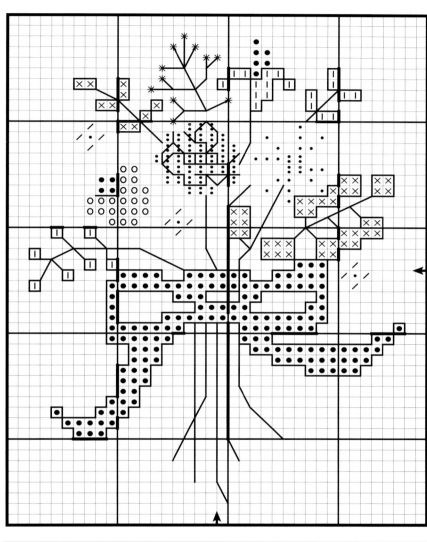

FLORAL BOUQUET

DMC	COLOR
∕ 828	blue, ultra light
∶ 353	peach flesh
• 677	old gold, very light
I 3348	yellow-green, light
X 3364	pine green
o 225	shell pink, very light
● 316	antique mauve, medium
bs 315	antique mauve, dark
bs 3363	pine green, medium
FK white	white

Fabric used for model: 12-count blue and white Arno from Wichelt Imports, Inc.
Stitch count: 44H x 34W
Approximate design size:
   12-count—3 ⅝" x 2 ⅞"
   14-count—3 ¼" x 2 ½"

Instructions: Cross stitch using two strands of floss. Backstitch using one strand of floss. Make French knots (FK) where symbol ∗ appears using two strands white, wrapping around needle twice.
Backstitch (bs) instructions:
   315   blossoms and ribbon
   3363   leaves and stems

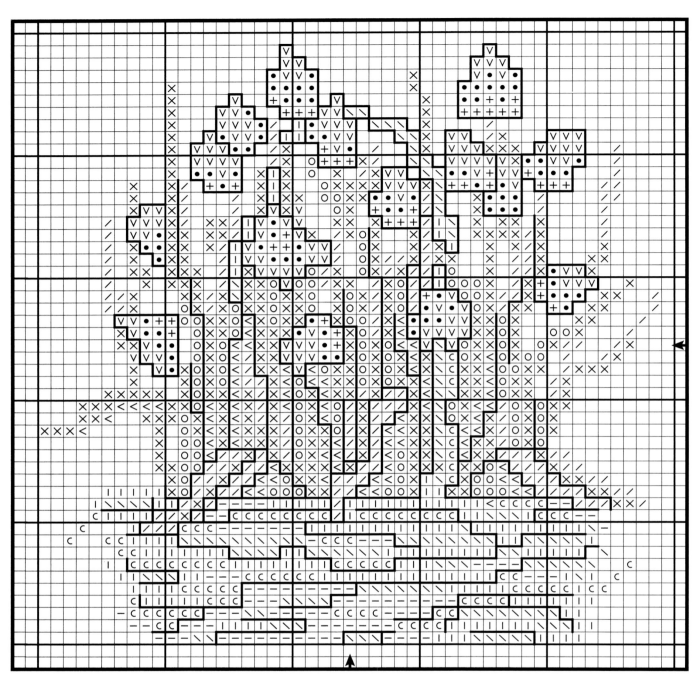

TULIP BASKET

	DMC	COLOR
V	745	yellow, light pale
•	977	golden brown, light
+	720	orange spice, dark
<	501	blue-green, dark
o	935	avocado green, dark
x	988	forest green, medium
/	471	avocado green, very light
−	898	coffee brown, very dark
I	433	brown, medium
\	435	brown, very light
c	437	tan, light

Fabric used for model: 14-count ivory Aida
Stitch count: 49H x 49W
Approximate design size:
    14-count—3 ½" x 3 ½"
    18-count—2 ¾" x 2 ¾"

Instructions: Cross stitch using two strands of floss. Backstitch using one strand of floss.
Backstitch (bs) instructions:
    435   tulips
    898   basket
    935   leaves

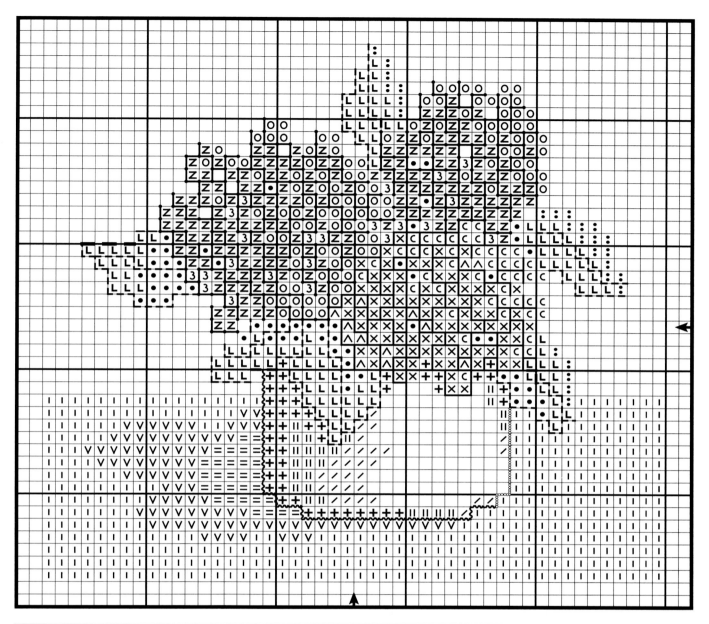

HYDRANGEA

	DMC	COLOR
=	743	yellow, medium
V	744	yellow, pale
I	744	yellow, pale (half cross)
+	453	shell gray, light
II	453	shell gray, light (half cross)
/	453	shell gray, light (half cross, one strand)
o	800	delft, pale
z	809	delft
3	799	delft, medium
c	3609	plum, ultra light (full cross, one strand)
x	3609	plum, ultra light
∧	3608	plum, very light
:	472	avocado green, ultra light
L	471	avocado green, very light
●	470	avocado green, light
bs	3607	plum, light
bs	452	shell gray, medium

Fabric used for model: 18-count white Aida
Stitch count: 43H x 48W

Approximate design size:
18-count—2 ½" x 2 ¾"

Instructions: Cross stitch using two strands of floss unless indicated otherwise. Backstitch using one strand of floss.
Backstitch (bs) instructions:
•••• 799
— 3607
∿∿ 452
∞∞ 453
---- 470

Floral Heart

Just a small corner of the bedroom is needed for this adorable, heart-shaped stool. Flowers have long been associated with love. With your needle in hand, you can stitch this permanent token of your affection for your sweetheart, or perhaps for your little girl.

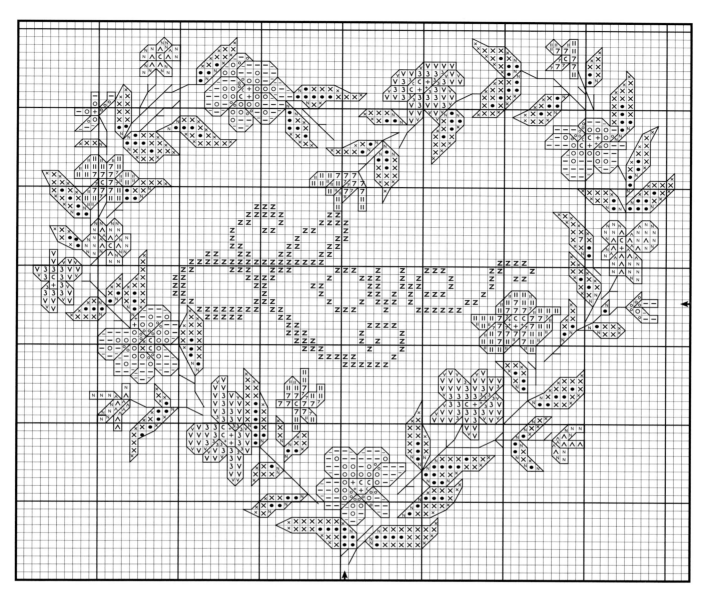

FLORAL HEART

DMC	COLOR
● 3346	hunter green
x 3347	yellow-green, medium
o 726	topaz, light
− 727	topaz, very light
3 813	blue, light
V 827	blue, very light
c 977	golden brown, light
+ 976	golden brown, medium
7 3326	rose, light
‖ 776	pink, medium

N 353	peach flesh
⋀ 352	coral, light
z 826	blue, medium
bs 3345	hunter green, dark
bs 725	topaz
bs 899	rose, medium
bs 351	coral

Fabric used for model: 32-count cream
Belfast linen from Zweigart®
Stitch count: 67H x 79W
Approximate design size:
14-count—4 ¾" x 5 ¾"

18-count—3 ¾" x 4 ½"
32-count—4 ¼" x 5"

Instructions: Cross stitch over two threads using two strands of floss. Backstitch using one strand of floss.
Backstitch (bs) instructions:

725	yellow flowers
899	pink flowers
826	blue flowers
351	peach flowers
976	flower centers
3345	flower stems and leaves

Flower Repeat

Create this simple flower design over and over again with oh-so-delicate shades of floss. Worked on three fabric counts, this stitchery demonstrates the subtle differences that can be achieved by varying the fabric used. Finish your efforts as a trio of dainty pillows, using trim from other sewing projects. This treatment is versatile and makes great use of small cross stitch fabric remnants and trims.

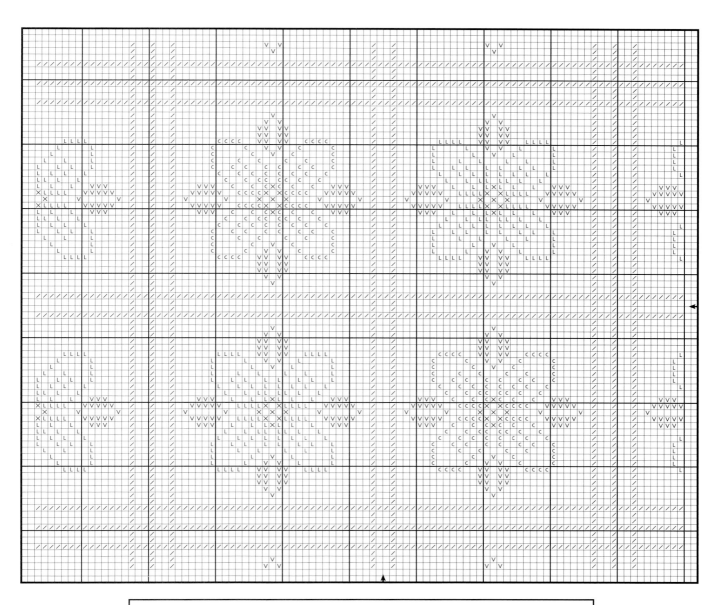

FLOWER REPEAT

	DMC	COLOR
c	3689	mauve, light
L	3688	mauve, medium
V	368	pistachio green, light
X	727	topaz, very light
/	3325	baby blue

Fabric used for models: 14-count white Aida; 8-count white Aida; and 11-count white Aida
Stitch count: 82H x 90W (one panel)

Approximate design size:
8-count—10 ¼" x 11 ¼"
11-count—7 ½" x 6 ⅜"
14-count—5 ⅞" x 6 ⅜"

Instructions: Cross stitch using two strands of floss on 14-count, four strands of floss on 8-count, and three strands of floss on 11-count. On 14-count, stitch block of four complete panels. On 8- and 11-counts, stitch one complete panel on each. Pillows were professionally finished. Turn to page 140 for finishing instructions.

Girl With Umbrella

Everyone loves to receive canning jars filled with jams, jellies, relishes, and pickles. To provide a fancy finishing touch to your tasty home-preserved gift, stitch *Girl With Umbrella* to use atop that jar bound for a country home's warm, inviting kitchen. Add a paper doily or a bit of lace under the jar ring, and your gift is ready to go!

GIRL WITH UMBRELLA

	DMC	COLOR
3	798	delft, dark
o	963	dusty rose, very light
I	794	cornflower blue, light
+	3078	golden yellow, very light
•	666	Christmas red, bright
■	3371	black-brown
⊙	962	dusty rose, medium
••	3348	yellow-green, light
8	3346	hunter green
7	3031	mocha brown, very dark
c	3047	yellow-beige, light
⁄	948	peach flesh, very light

Fabric used for model: 22-count dresden blue Oslo from Zweigart®
Stitch count: 62H x 52W
Approximate design size:
    14-count—4 ½" x 3 ¾"
    18-count—3 ½" x 2 ⅞"
    22-count—2 ¾" x 2 ⅜"

Instructions: Cross stitch over one thread using two strands of floss. Backstitch using one strand of floss. **Note:** Circular outline for placement only. Turn to page 140 for finishing instructions.
Backstitch (bs) instructions:
    798   puddle
    3346   flower stems and leaves
    3371   remainder of backstitching

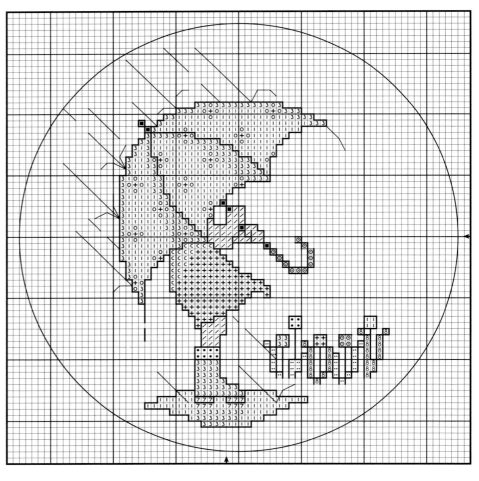

Weather Vane

Make a spot for yourself in someone's heart when you present this clever weather vane with warm wishes for sunny days and moonlit nights. The rooster is worked in floss colors that duplicate the metal used for real-life weather vanes, and the four corner motifs offer a sampling of stitches.

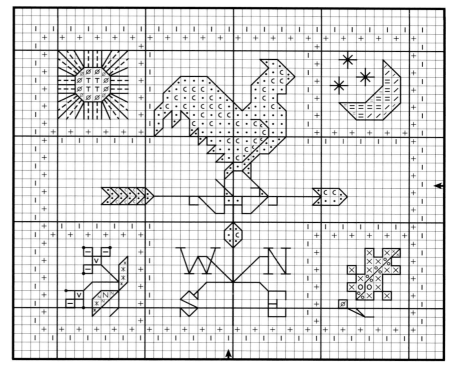

WEATHER VANE

	DMC	COLOR
V	209	lavender, dark
=	318	steel gray, light
•	413	pewter gray, dark
c	414	steel gray, dark
⁄	415	pearl gray
T	725	topaz
o	732	olive green
x	734	olive green, light
∅	783	Christmas gold
ı	930	antique blue, dark
+	931	antique blue, medium
−	3326	rose, light
N	3347	yellow-green, medium
*	3348	yellow-green, light

Fabric used for model: 25-count Floba® from Zweigart®
Stitch count: 37H x 45W
Approximate design size:
    14-count—2 ¾" x 3 ¼"
    18-count—2 ¼" x 2 ½"
    25-count—3" x 3 ⅝"

Instructions: Cross stitch over two threads using two strands of floss. Backstitch using one strand of floss unless indicated otherwise. Make French knots on flowers using two strands 725, wrapping around needle twice.
Backstitch (bs) instructions:
413	weather vane (two strands), rooster
725	sun and sun's rays indicated with broken line
783	sun's rays indicated with solid lines, leaf and acorn
414	flower, moon
415	stars (next to moon)

Hearts In The Round

Hidden away beneath this quartet of pastel hearts, inside a tiny trinket box, are Grandmother's sweet treats that she brings out at just the right time. This oh-so-feminine stitchery is sure to bring memories of those days from your childhood spent with Grandma. Stitch this design for use atop a trinket box for your grandmother, or stitch for your little girl for her cherished possessions. Perhaps when she's a grandmother, she'll carry on the tradition of sharing tasty delectables with her favorite little ones.

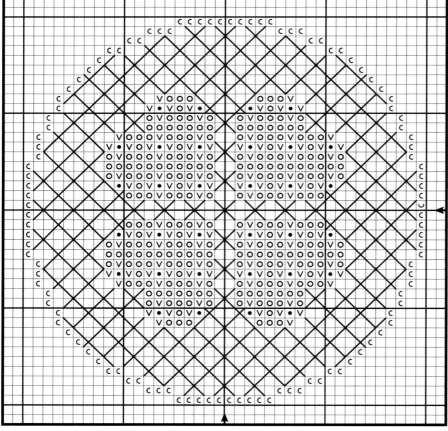

HEARTS IN THE ROUND

	DMC	COLOR
o	776	pink, medium
V	813	blue, light
•	744	yellow, pale
c	913	nile green, medium
bs	955	nile green, light

Fabric used for model: 14-count white Aida

Stitch count: 40H x 40W

Approximate design size:
14-count—2 ⅞" x 2 ⅞"
18-count—2 ¼" x 2 ¼"

Instructions: Cross stitch using three strands of floss. Backstitch (bs) using one strand 955.

Autumn's Gift

Anyone who loves curling up with a good book will appreciate this pretty, as well as practical gift. By simply adding your stitches to a pre-finished bookmark, you can create this harvesttime charmer for your favorite bookworm.

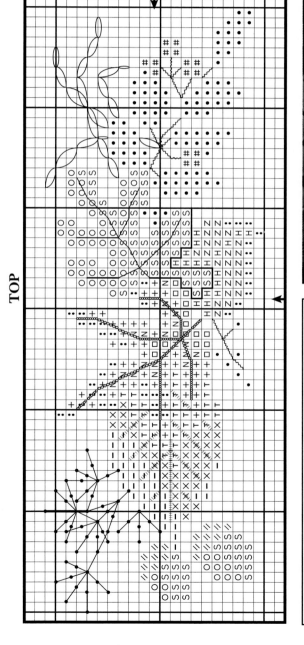

AUTUMN'S GIFT

	DMC	COLOR
o	435	brown, very light
s	434	brown, light
// [	434	brown, light and
	898	coffee brown, very dark
□	350	coral, medium
N	352	coral, light
+ [	352	coral, light and
	726	topaz, light
:	726	topaz, light
●	902	garnet, very dark
#	720	orange spice, dark
H	783	Christmas gold
z	725	topaz
T	919	red-copper
x	920	copper, medium
—	921	copper
·	550	violet, very dark

Fabric used for model: 18-count ecru pre-finished Continental Collection bookmark from Craft World®, Inc.

Stitch count: 21H x 60W

Approximate design size:
14-count—1 ½" x 4 ¼"
18-count—1 ¼" x 3 ⅜"

Instructions: Cross stitch using two strands of floss. Backstitch using one strand of floss. When two colors are bracketed together, use one strand of each.

Backstitch (bs) instructions:
ᴧᴧᴧ 898
◠◠ 680
— 801
ıllıl 918
•••• 3052
◇◇◇◇ 732

Gifts
For Special People

Handmade gifts have a winning way of conveying warm feelings of love. For those important people in your life, from babies and school-age children to dear friends, stitch the gifts pictured on the following pages.

When This I See

Art aprons for your little ones show off your handiwork while protecting their clothing and keeping their art supplies close at hand. For girls, a round-top bib trimmed with eyelet is adorned with the *ABC* design. Little boys will prefer the straight lines of an apron patterned after Dad's cookout apron. A portion of the design *When This I See* is stitched on the boy's apron. Pencils, crayons, rulers and ABCs define the simple sampler which will serve as a reminder of those early school years.

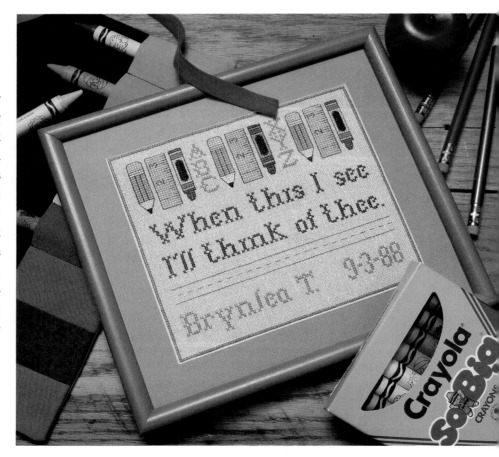

47

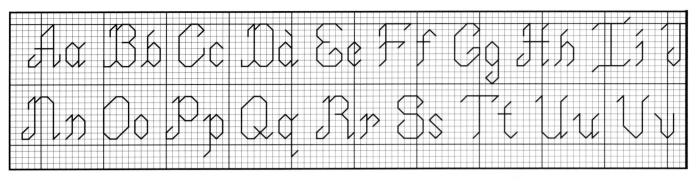

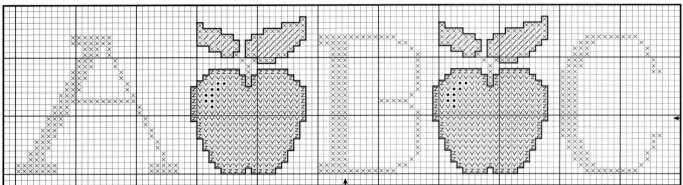

A B C		
	DMC	COLOR
V	498	Christmas red, dark
•	746	off white
z	815	garnet, medium
x	3345	hunter green, dark
⁄	3346	hunter green
bs	3371	black-brown
bs	792	cornflower blue, dark

Fabric used for model: 14-count ivory Aida on apron from Lollipop Designs
Stitch count: 35H x 109W
Approximate design size:
   14-count—2 ½" x 7 ⅞"
   18-count—2" x 6 ⅛"

Instructions: Cross stitch using two strands of floss. Backstitch using two strands of floss. **Note:** Design may be personalized using alphabet given.
Backstitch (bs) instructions:
   792   tablet line
   3371   apples, leaves

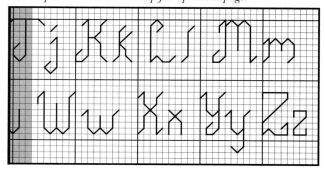

Personalization Chart For *When This I See*

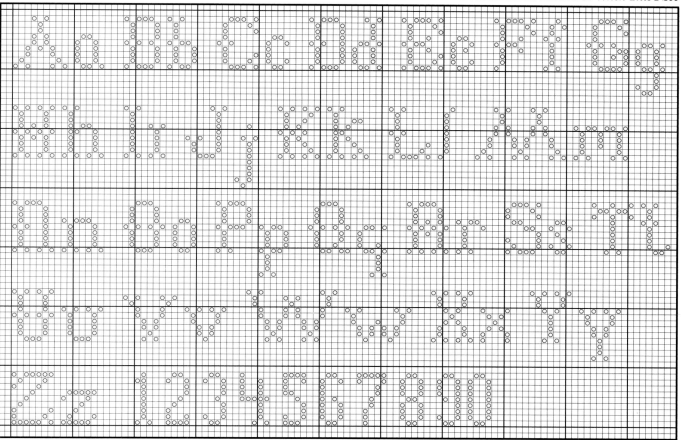

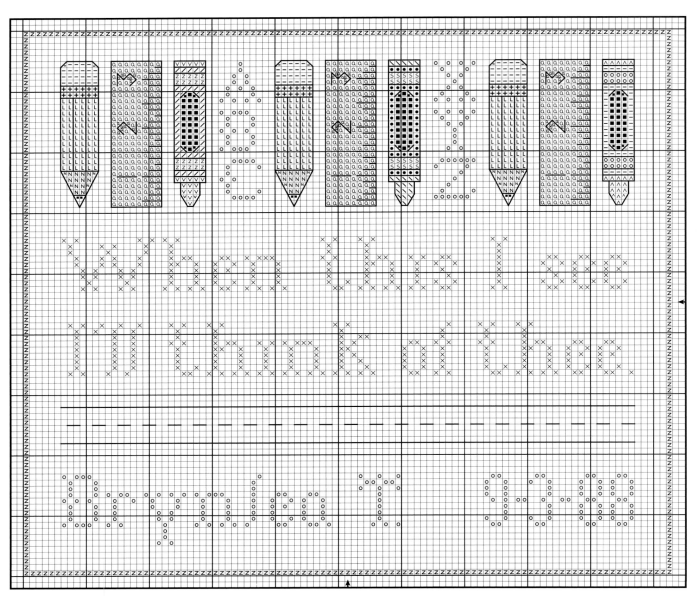

WHEN THIS I SEE		
DMC	**COLOR**	
V	312	navy blue, light
z	322	navy blue, very light
∧	355	terra cotta, dark
o	356	terra cotta, medium
N	739	tan, ultra light
–	758	terra cotta, light
+	762	pearl gray, very light
L	783	Christmas gold
\	986	forest green, very dark
s	987	forest green, dark
•	989	forest green

■	3371	black-brown
/	3325	baby blue
x	801	coffee brown, dark
ɑ	437	tan, light
bs	938	coffee brown, ultra dark

Fabric used for model: 29-count natural Glenshee linen from Anne Powell, Ltd.

Stitch count: 90H x 103W

Approximate design size:
14-count—6 ½" x 7 ⅜"
18-count—5" x 5 ¾"
29-count—6 ¼" x 7 ⅛"

Instructions: Cross stitch over two threads using two strands of floss. Backstitch using two strands of floss unless indicated otherwise.

Backstitch (bs) instructions:
322   tablet lines
938   remainder of backstitching (one strand)

Tin Can Treasures

Display your cross stitch on tin cans and wait for rave reviews from the children in your life. They will love selecting a sweet treat from the *Lollipop Shop*! *Late For School* transforms an ordinary metal can into an attractive pencil holder—a handy desk accessory for student or teacher!

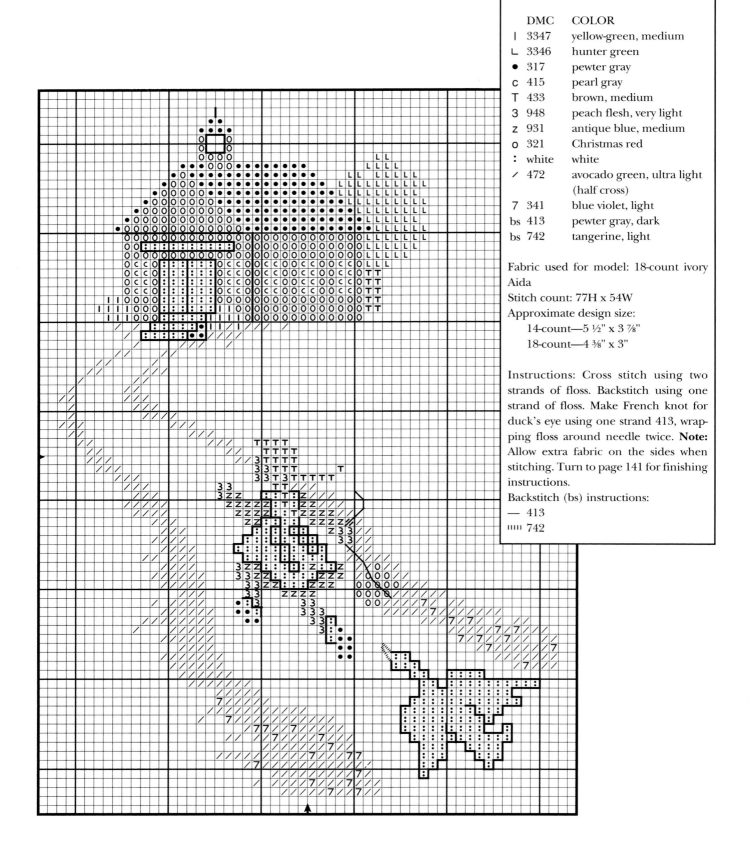

LATE FOR SCHOOL

	DMC	COLOR
I	3347	yellow-green, medium
L	3346	hunter green
●	317	pewter gray
c	415	pearl gray
T	433	brown, medium
3	948	peach flesh, very light
z	931	antique blue, medium
o	321	Christmas red
:	white	white
/	472	avocado green, ultra light (half cross)
7	341	blue violet, light
bs	413	pewter gray, dark
bs	742	tangerine, light

Fabric used for model: 18-count ivory Aida
Stitch count: 77H x 54W
Approximate design size:
    14-count—5 ½" x 3 ⅞"
    18-count—4 ⅜" x 3"

Instructions: Cross stitch using two strands of floss. Backstitch using one strand of floss. Make French knot for duck's eye using one strand 413, wrapping floss around needle twice. **Note:** Allow extra fabric on the sides when stitching. Turn to page 141 for finishing instructions.
Backstitch (bs) instructions:
— 413
ııııı 742

LOLLIPOP SHOP

	DMC	COLOR
c	321	Christmas red
z	356	terra cotta, medium
3	743	yellow, medium
L	702	kelly green
o	806	peacock blue, dark
=	552	violet, dark
x	435	brown, very light
bs	413	pewter gray, dark

Fabric used for model: 14-count white Aida
Stitch count: 39H x 75W
Approximate design size:
    14-count—2 ⅞" x 5 ⅜"
    18-count—2 ¼" x 4 ¼"

Instructions: Cross stitch using two strands of floss. Backstitch using two strands 413.
Finishing: Allow extra fabric on the sides when stitching. Turn to "General Finishing Instructions".

Mirror Image

Under an arc of country-bright hearts, two little girls sit back to back beneath sheltering sunbonnets. This old-fashioned design, stitched on white Aida, is a natural for today's country decor, which calls to mind images of sunbonnet days, grandmother's iron bed, handmade quilts, pitchers and wash bowls, and lace-edged linens.

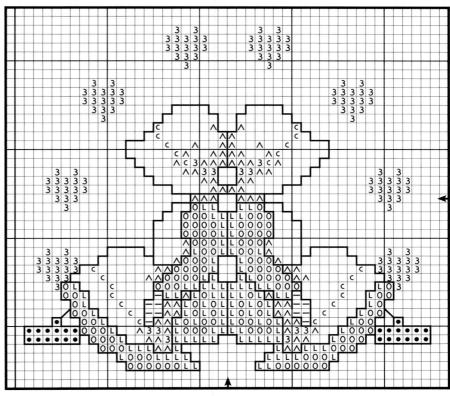

MIRROR IMAGE

	DMC	COLOR
●	938	coffee brown, ultra dark
∧	415	pearl gray
o	932	antique blue, light
L	931	antique blue, medium
c	3688	mauve, medium
3	3687	mauve
−	951	sportsman flesh, very light
bs	938	coffee brown, ultra dark

Fabric used for model: 14-count white Aida
Stitch count: 39H x 44W
Approximate design size:
    14-count—2 ⅞" x 3 ¼"
    18-count—2 ¼" x 2 ½"

Instructions: Cross stitch using three strands
of floss. Backstitch using one strand 938.

Lunchtime Pals

Is there a better way to welcome a new arrival than with a gift from your hands? Babies will love the bright colors, and moms will appreciate the beauty of your very practical gift! Stitch several while vacationing. Just tuck the floss and bibs into your tote and take advantage of travel time for quick projects. When the baby shower is announced, your gift will be ready! If little ones visit you often, keep a couple of bibs handy for them to use during quick snacks and lunch dates.

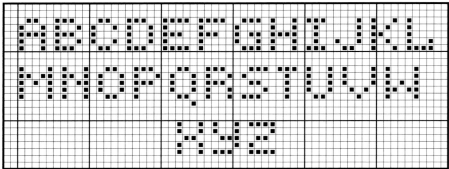

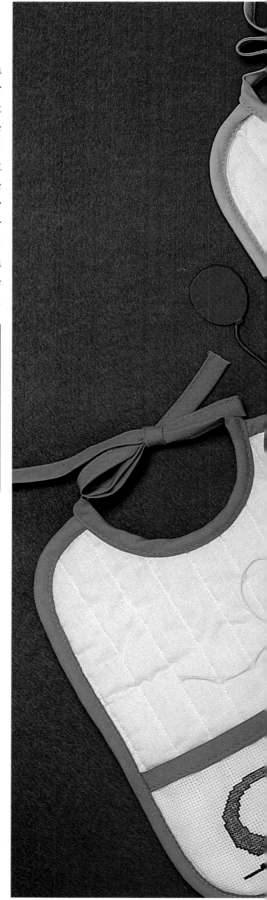

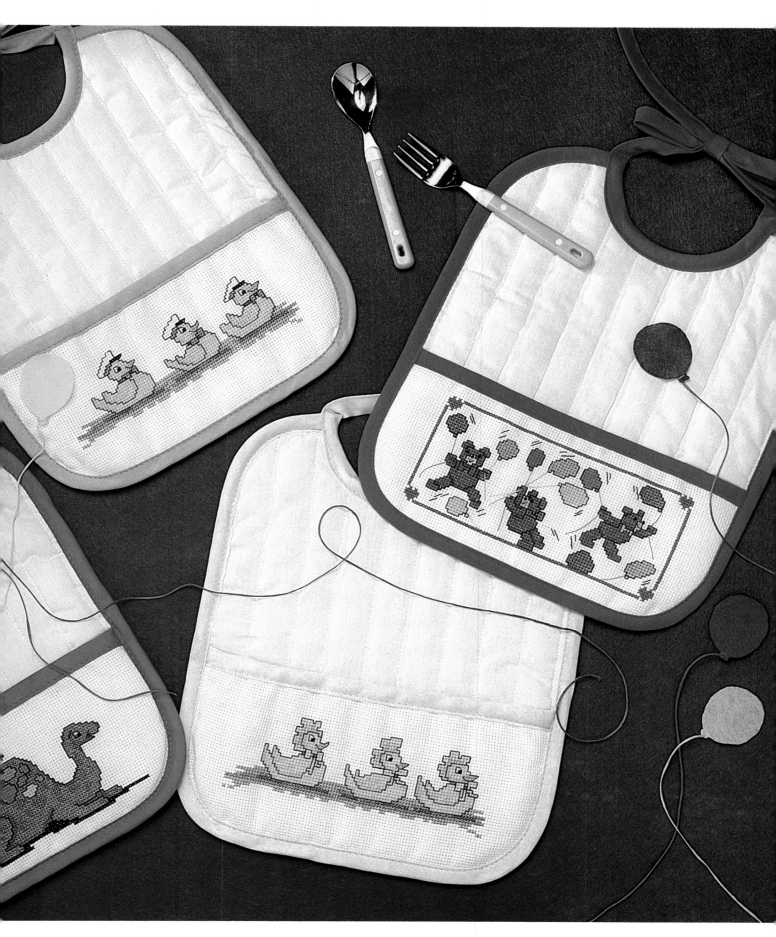

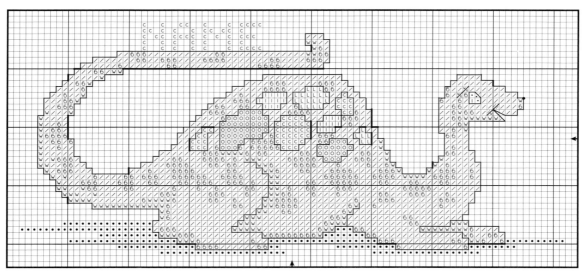

DINO-BABY

	DMC	COLOR
⁄	702	kelly green
6	701	Christmas green, light
w	700	Christmas green, bright
●	310	black
•	white	white

o	973	canary, bright
c	891	carnation, dark
I	518	wedgewood, light
L	970	pumpkin, light

Fabric used for model: 14-count white quilted bib with green trim from The Janlynn Corporation

Stitch count: 40H x 90W
Approximate design size:
14-count—2 ⅞" x 6 ½"

Instructions: Cross stitch using two strands of floss. Backstitch (bs) using one strand 310. Make French knot for nose using two strands 310, wrapping around needle twice.

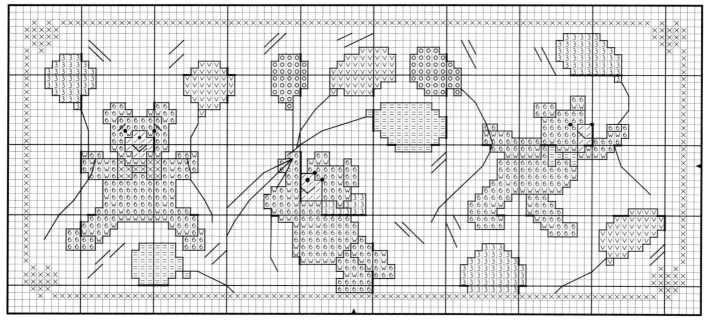

BALLOONS 'N TEDDIES

	DMC	COLOR
w	433	brown, medium
6	434	brown, light
⁄	437	tan, light
3	826	blue, medium
o	350	coral, medium
=	444	lemon, dark
V	704	chartreuse, bright

x	349	coral, dark
bs	3371	black-brown

Fabric used for model: 14-count white quilted bib with red trim from The Janlynn Corporation
Stitch count: 40H x 90W
Approximate design size:
14-count—2 ⅞" x 6 ½"

Instructions: Cross stitch using two strands of floss. Backstitch (bs) using one strand 3371. Straight stitch each balloon string in the color of the balloon using one strand of floss. Make French knots for eyes and noses using two strands 3371, wrapping around needle twice.

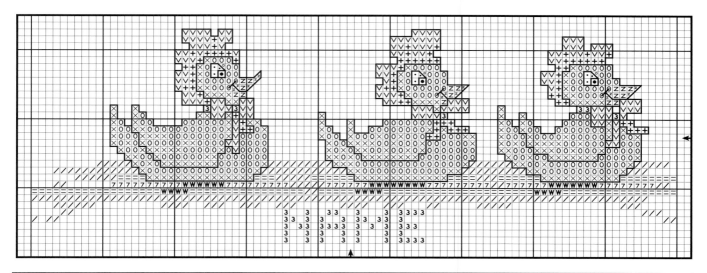

DUCKLINGS—FOR LITTLE GIRLS

DMC	COLOR			
• white	white	z	741	tangerine, medium
• 3371	black-brown	x	444	lemon, dark
∕ 809	delft	o	307	lemon
= 799	delft, medium	V	605	cranberry, very light
7 798	delft, dark	+	604	cranberry, light
w [798	delft, dark and	3	602	cranberry, medium
[741	tangerine, medium			

Fabric used for model: 14-count white quilted bib with pink trim from The Janlynn Corporation

Stitch count: 31H x 90W
Approximate design size:
14-count—2 ¼" x 6 ½"

Instructions: Cross stitch using two strands of floss. Backstitch (bs) using one strand 3371. When two colors are bracketed together, use one strand of each. Option: Symbol ∕ may be worked in a half cross instead of a full cross, if desired.

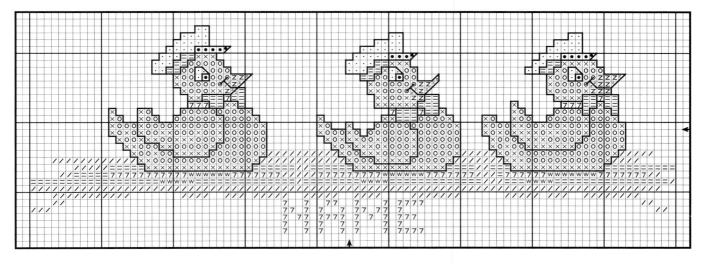

DUCKLINGS—FOR LITTLE BOYS

DMC	COLOR			
• white	white	x	444	lemon, dark
• 3371	black-brown	o	307	lemon
∕ 809	delft	w [798		delft, dark
= 799	delft, medim	[741		tangerine, medium
7 798	delft, dark			
z 741	tangerine, medium			

Fabric used for model: 14-count white quilted bib with blue trim from The Janlynn Corporation
Stitch count: 30H x 90W

Approximate design size:
14-count—2 ¼" x 6 ½ "

Instructions: Cross stitch using two strands of floss. Backstitch (bs) using one strand 3371. When two colors are bracketed together, use one strand of each. Option: Symbol ∕ may be worked in a half cross instead of full cross if desired.

Skipping Rope

Remember when a sunny afternoon included skipping rope with friends? Whether your favorite was singles, doubles, snakes, or high-wire, you'll enjoy stitching this nostalgic design, even if you've long ago hung up your jump rope. Give this gift to a new generation skipper, or to an older friend who shares fond memories of those afternoons spent skipping rope.

SKIPPING ROPE

	DMC	COLOR
●	310	black
:	677	old gold, very light
o	676	old gold, light
L	729	old gold, medium
•	948	peach flesh, very light
c	951	sportsman flesh, very light
‖	225	shell pink, very light
7	762	pearl gray, very light
╱	453	shell gray, light (half cross)
=	3688	mauve, medium
3	3687	mauve
z	3685	mauve, dark
x	801	coffee brown, dark
bs	3328	salmon, medium

Fabric used for model: 18-count white Aida

Stitch count: 55H x 45W

Approximate design size:
    14-count—3 ⅞" x 3 ¼"
    18-count—3" x 2 ½"

Instructions: Cross stitch using two strands of floss. Backstitch using one strand of floss unless indicated otherwise.

Backstitch (bs) instructions:
▬ 310
∿∿ 951   nose (two strands)
--- 453
∞∞∞ 3328   mouth

Geometric Pincushion

The collecting of antique needlework tools is at an all-time high for avid stitchers. This pincushion, with its pastel pattern and tassel, brings back memories of a bygone era. This design can be easily adapted to table linens, and will lend an elegant touch to linen place mats. Position the design in the upper left-hand corner of each place mat, and select floss colors to match your china.

GEOMETRIC PINCUSHION

	DMC	COLOR
c	502	blue green
x	503	blue green, medium
∧	504	blue green, light
I	211	lavender, light
-	519	sky blue
+	963	dusty rose, very light
o	3078	golden yellow, very light

Fabric used for model: 18-count white Aida

Stitch count: 49H x 49W

Approximate design size:

14-count—3 ½" x 3 ½"

18-count—2 ¾" x 2 ¾"

Instructions: Cross stitch using two strands of floss. Turn to page 140 for finishing instructions. (See pillow finishing instructions.)

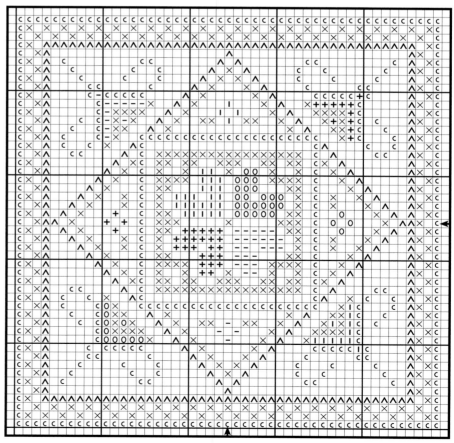

SIT WITH ME

	DMC	COLOR
−	white	white
•	962	dusty rose, medium
■	904	parrot green, very dark
+	819	baby blue, light
bs	3685	mauve, dark
bs	906	parrot green, medium

Fabric used for model: 14-count ivory Aida
Stitch count: 39H x 77W
Approximate design size:
    14-count—2 ⅝" x 5 ½"
    18-count—2 ¼" x 4 ⅜"

Instructions: Cross stitch using two strands
of floss. Backstitch using two strands of floss
unless indicated otherwise.

Backstitch (bs) instructions:
  906   pink flowers (one strand)
  3685   cups, saucers, and steam
  904   remainder of backstitching

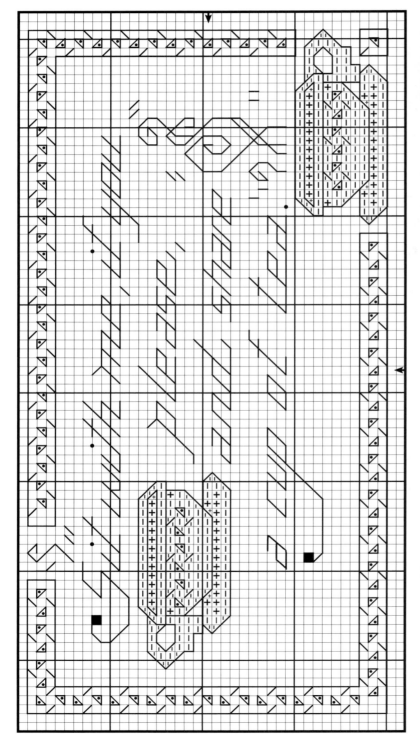

Sit With Me

For aficionados of all things English, afternoon tea has become an important part of today's lifestyle, as it was years ago. This easily accomplished piece, worked primarily in backstitch, will provide the perfect backdrop to this daily ritual.

Trusted Friend Sampler

This sampler's sentiment, found among the letters of the alphabet, expresses the feeling shared by many—friends are one of the wonderful blessings of life. Personalize the gift by stitching your initials, the year, and your friend's initials.

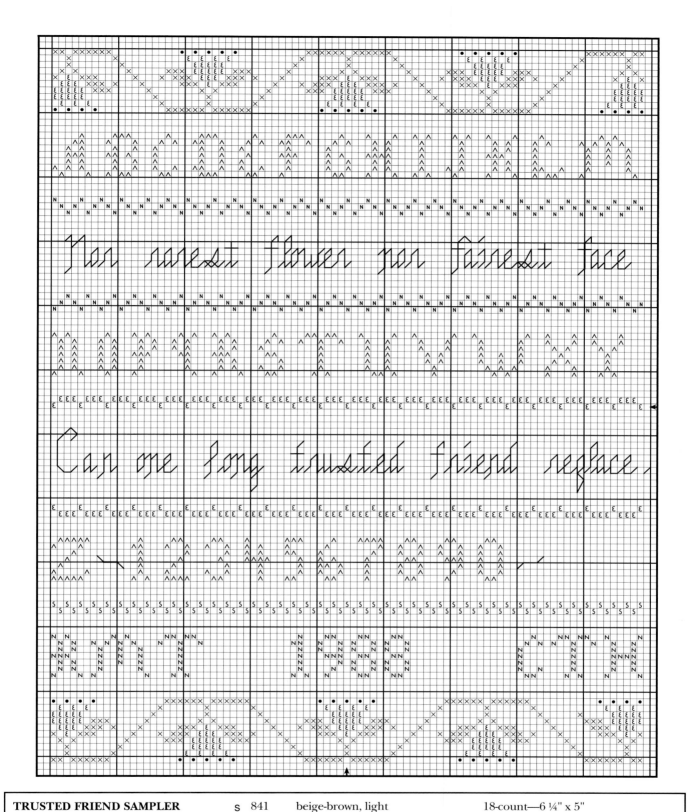

TRUSTED FRIEND SAMPLER

	DMC	COLOR
x	319	pistachio green, very dark
●	355	terra cotta, dark
ε	758	terra cotta, light
∧	930	antique blue, dark
s	841	beige-brown, light
N	931	antique blue, medium

Fabric used for model: 26-count golden flax linen from Wichelt Imports, Inc.
Stitch count: 111H x 89W
Approximate design size:
    14-count—8" x 6⅝"

18-count—6¼" x 5"
26-count—7⅞" x 6⅝"

Instructions: Cross stitch over two threads using two strands of floss. Backstitch lettering using one strand 355.

The World's Best

Ideal for a dentist friend, this design will bring smiles from his patients when he displays it prominently in his office. A complete alphabet and charts for a variety of professions, from jewelers to pharmacists to teachers, are included. Your Very Important Person will be delighted with lasting mementos of your affection.

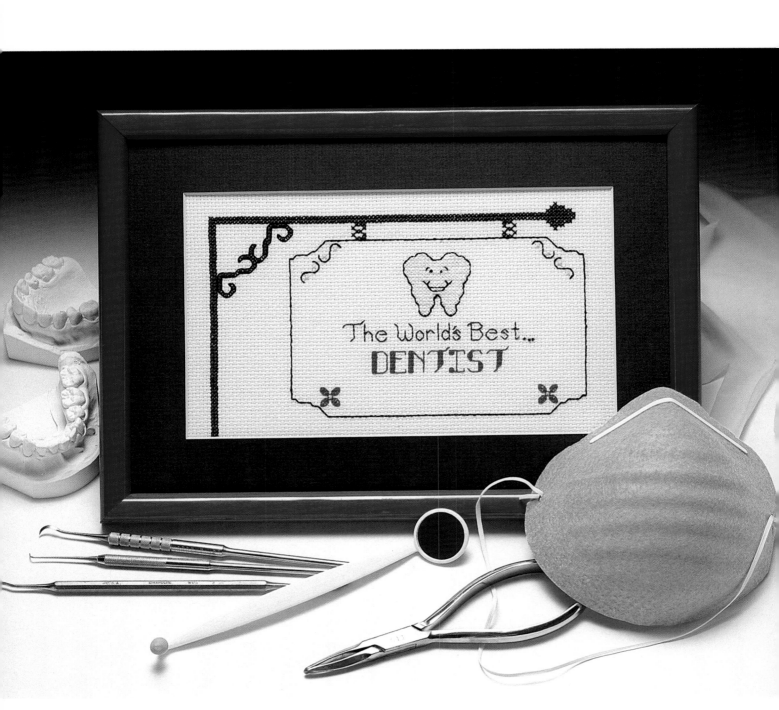

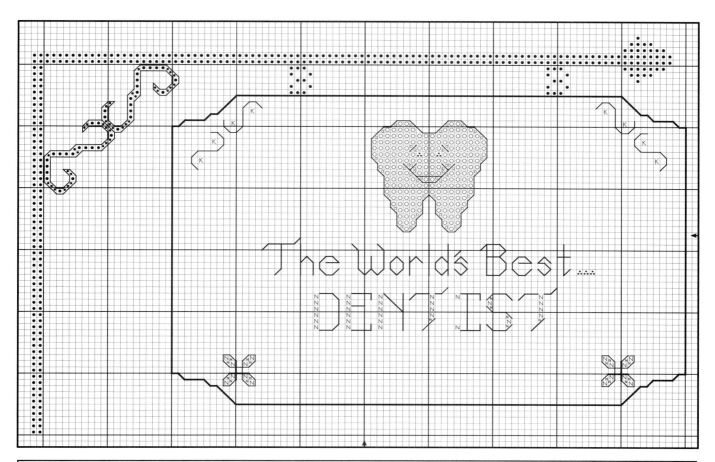

THE WORLD'S BEST

	DMC	COLOR
o	white	white
J	415	pearl gray
x	310	black
●	336	navy blue
=	608	bright orange
+	775	baby blue, light
N	817	coral red, very dark
s	312	navy blue, light
L	581	moss green
△	781	topaz, dark
K	726	topaz, light
-	948	peach flesh, very light
ε	801	coffee brown, dark
<	904	parrot green, very dark
8	783	Christmas gold
e	304	Christmas red, medium
\	470	avocado green, light
FK	336	navy blue

Fabric used for model: 14-count antique white Aida from Charles Craft, Inc.
Stitch count: 65H x 102W
Approximate design size:
   14-count—4 ⅝" x 7 ¼"
   18-count—3 ⅝" x 5 ⅝"

Instructions: Cross stitch using two strands of floss. Backstitch using one strand of floss. Make French knots where symbol ⁙ appears using two strands 336, wrapping around needle twice. **Note**: Select design and title of your choice and center above and below lettering respectively.
Backstitch instructions:

312	*The World's Best*
817	alphabet, flowers in corners of sign
310	remainder of backstitching

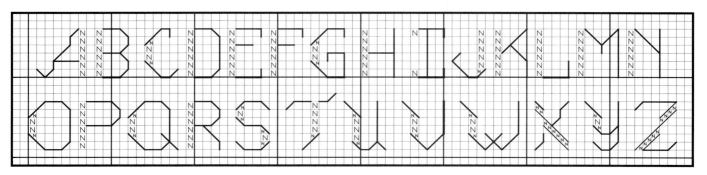

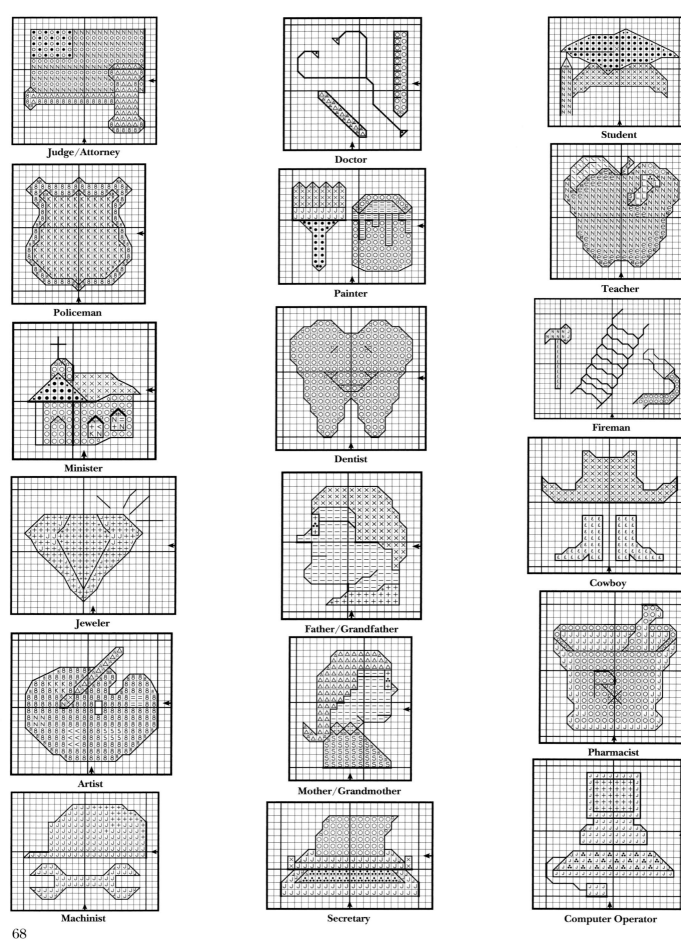

Judge/Attorney

Doctor

Student

Policeman

Painter

Teacher

Minister

Dentist

Fireman

Jeweler

Father/Grandfather

Cowboy

Artist

Mother/Grandmother

Pharmacist

Machinist

Secretary

Computer Operator

Posey Alphabet

This trio of complementary alphabets, charted in three different sizes, will allow you to mix and match letters in a variety of combinations. Use for personalizing an array of gift items. Monogrammed hand towels make lovely shower gifts, and your stitching friends will surely welcome personalized scissors cases. Sachet bags make wonderful stocking stuffers and last-minute gifts, but they can also be used to wrap small items, making the wrapping an important part of the gift which will be remembered long after traditional paper and bows have been discarded. With your imagination, the possibilities are endless!

SMALL ALPHABET

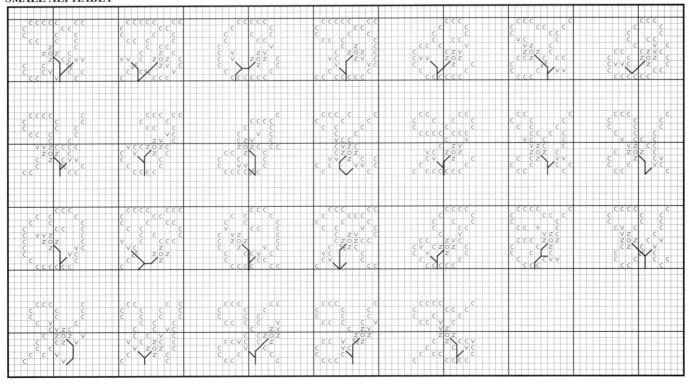

POSEY ALPHABET

DMC		COLOR
c	793	cornflower blue, medium
V	503	blue green, medium
o	676	old gold, light
x	224	shell pink, light
z	223	shell pink, medium
©	793	cornflower blue, medium

Fabric used for models: 14-count cream small, medium, and large scissor cases; 14-count white Aida tissue holder; and 27-count off white sachet bag from The Janlynn Corporation; 14-count ecru/weathered tan twill Borderlines Fingertips towel from Charles Craft, Inc.; 18-count cream pre-finished Continental Collection bookmark from Craft World®, Inc.
Stitch count: Large Alphabet—20H x 20W, Medium Alphabet—15H x 15W, Small Alphabet—10H x 10W
Approximate design size:
Scissor Cases
Large Alphabet
14-count—1 ⅜" x 1 ⅜"
Medium Alphabet
14-count—1 ⅛" x 1 ⅛"
Small Alphabet
14-count—¾" x ¾"
Tissue Holder (small alphabet)
Sachet bag (large alphabet)
27-count—1 ½" x 1 ½"
Borderlines Fingertips towel
(large alphabet)
Bookmark (small alphabet)
18-count—½" x ½"

Instructions: Cross stitch using three strands of floss. Backstitch using two strands 503. **Note:** The color 793 has two symbols. This is correct.

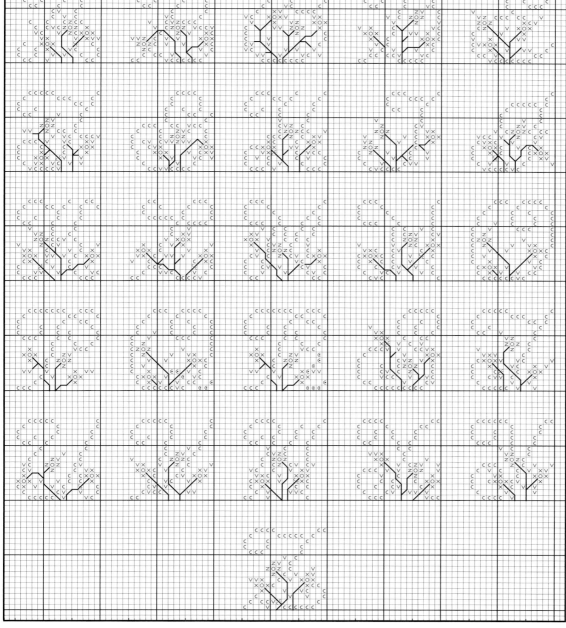

MEDIUM ALPHABET

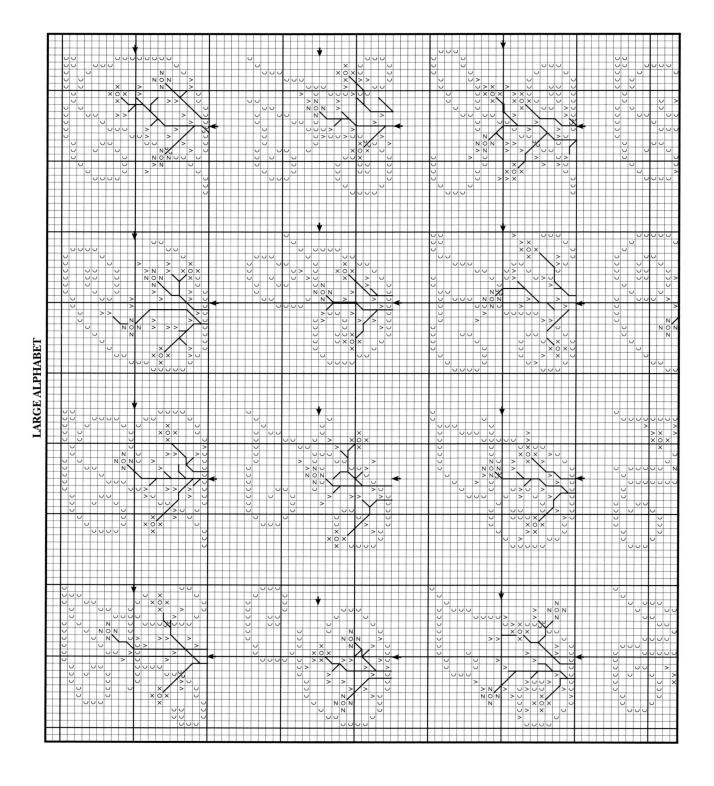

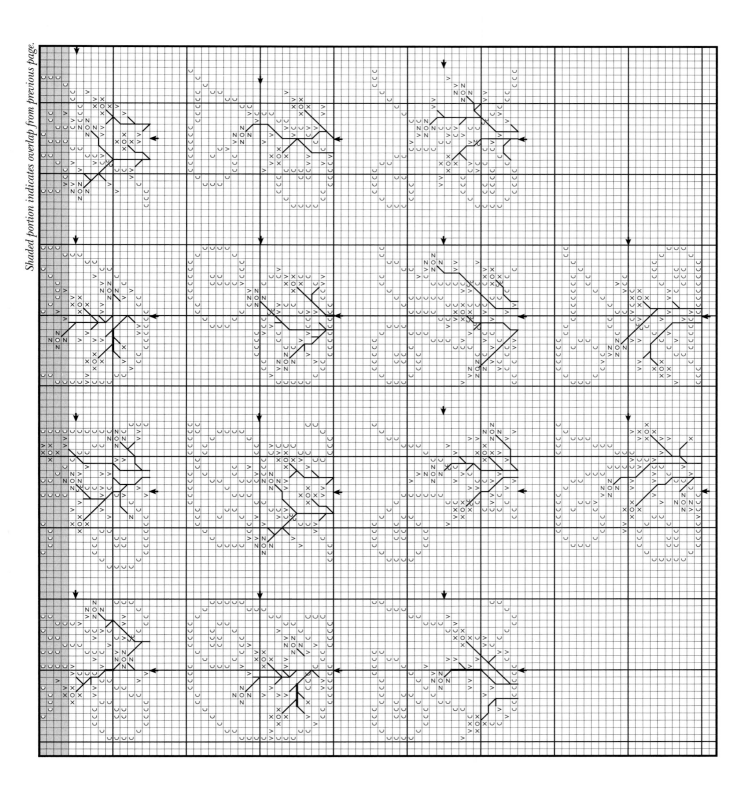

Miles Apart– Close At Heart

Present this adorable design to a college student who's leaving home for the first time, or to a neighbor who's moving. As she settles into her new home, she'll appreciate the heartfelt message which is sure to remind her of family and dear friends who are across the miles, but as close as a phone call.

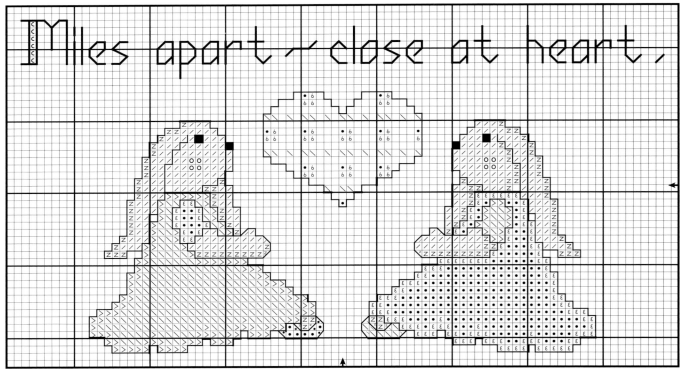

MILES APART—CLOSE AT HEART			■	844	beaver gray, ultra dark	Instructions: Cross stitch over two threads

	DMC	COLOR
z	842	beige-brown, very light
⁄	543	beige-brown, ultra light
o	761	salmon, light
>	793	cornflower blue, medium
\	794	cornflower blue, light
ε	223	shell pink, medium
•	224	shell pink, light

■	844	beaver gray, ultra dark
c	792	cornflower blue, dark
6	677	old gold, very light

Fabric used for model: 27-count ivory linen from Norden Crafts
Stitch count: 46H x 85W
Approximate design size:
    27-count—3 ⅜" x 6 ¼"

Instructions: Cross stitch over two threads using two strands of floss. Backstitch using one strand of floss unless otherwise indicated.
Backstitch (bs) instructions:

844	rabbits, hearts
792	lettering (two strands)

Two For Tea

A Victorian woman's home was her prized possession, and great efforts went into establishing customs that would be carried on for generations to come. Entertaining was done in the home, and the ceremony of having afternoon tea with friends and acquaintances was very important. This stitched piece captures the spirit of afternoon tea, and will be a treasured gift for a sipping companion.

TWO FOR TEA

	DMC	COLOR
z	822	beige-gray, light
╱	746	off white
x	794	cornflower blue, light
▪	221	shell pink, dark
—	225	shell pink, very light
•	502	blue green
I	3024	brown-gray, very light
N	white	white
o	224	pink, light
bs	645	beaver gray, very dark

Fabric used for model: 27-count ivory linen from Norden Crafts
Stitch count: 56H x 71W
Approximate design size:
    27-count—4 ⅛" x 5 ¼"

Instructions: Cross stitch over two threads using two strands of floss. Backstitch using one strand 645.

A Friend

A good friend is a precious gift, and yours will know how much you value the relationship you share when she unwraps this colorful fancywork wrought by your hands. Inspired by intricate quilt designs, the borders and verses are interchangeable.

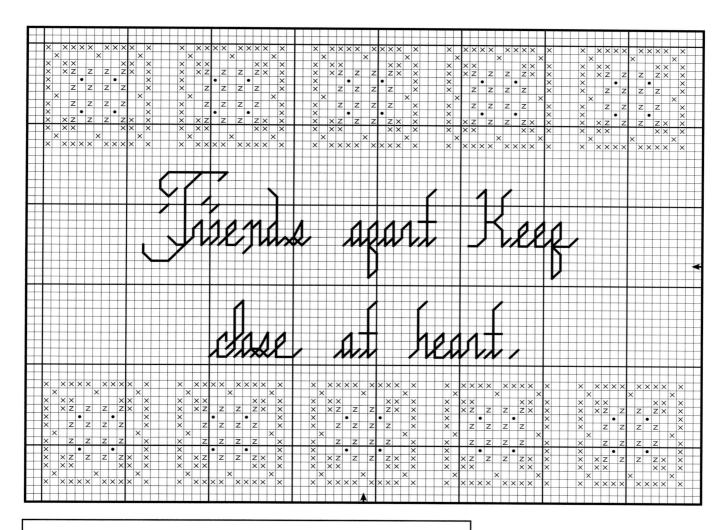

A FRIEND			Stitch count: 55H x 77W
			Approximate design size:
	DMC	COLOR	14-count—4" x 5 ½"
x	502	blue-green	18-count—3" x 4 ¼"
z	760	salmon	
•	761	salmon, light	Instructions: Cross stitch using two strands of floss. Backstitch (bs) using two strands 840.
bs	840	beige-brown, medium	

Fabric used for model: 14-count antique white Aida from Charles Craft, Inc.

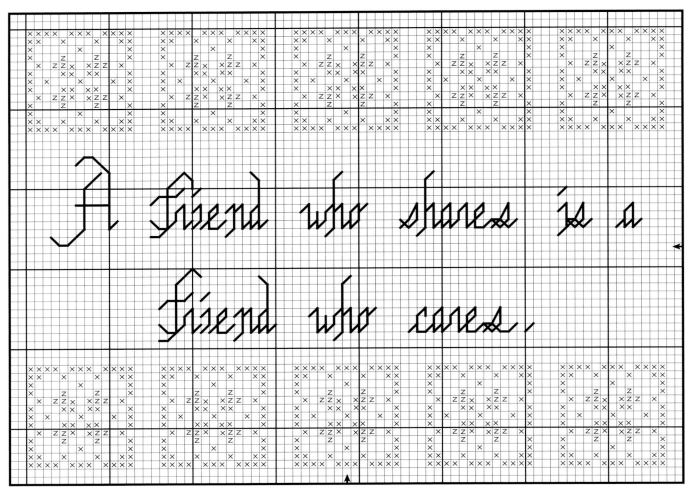

(Color code has been duplicated from previous page for stitching convenience.)

A FRIEND

	DMC	COLOR
x	502	blue-green
z	760	salmon
•	761	salmon, light
bs	840	beige-brown, medium

Fabric used for model: 14-count antique white Aida from Charles Craft, Inc.

Stitch count: 55H x 77W
Approximate design size:
    14-count—4" x 5 ½"
    18-count—3" x 4 ¼"

Instructions: Cross stitch using two strands of floss. Backstitch (bs) using two strands 840.

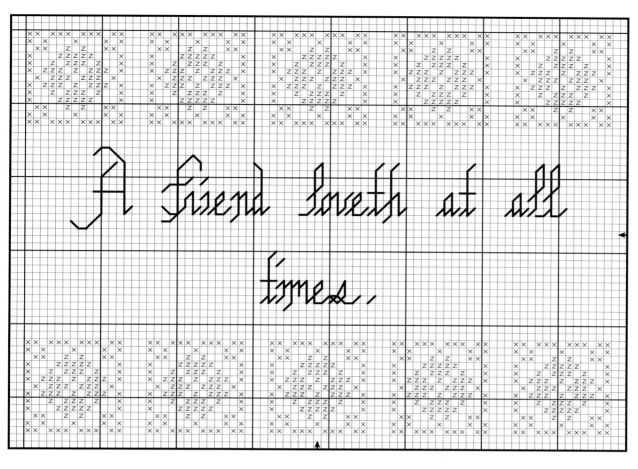

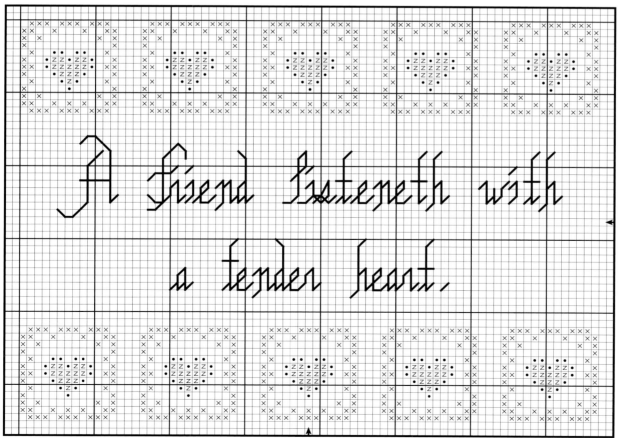

Blessed Are The Piece-makers

Classic quilt-block patterns and a quaint verse for quilters make this an ideal gift for all your quilting friends. For added variety, stitch the quilt square motifs alone on the bands of hand towels, or work a favorite block pattern separately for use as a box topper.

BLESSED ARE THE PIECE-MAKERS		
	DMC	COLOR
x	223	shell pink, medium
o	502	blue green
bs	640	beige-gray, very dark
bs	318	steel gray, light

Fabric used for model: 14-count cream Aida

Stitch count: 31H x 73W

Approximate design size:
    14-count—2 ¼" x 5 ¼"
    18-count—1 ¾" x 4 ⅛"

Instructions: Cross stitch using two strands of floss. Backstitch using one strand of floss unless indicated otherwise.

Backstitch (bs) instructions:
ᨊᨊᨊ 318   (two strands)
—   640   remainder of backstitching

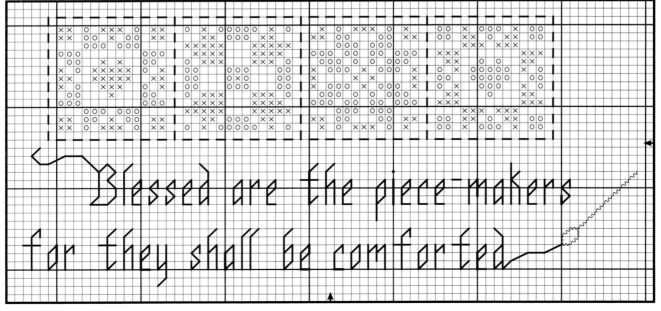

He Who Indulges Bulges

This adorable porker, who has plopped himself down on a bed of flowers to munch contentedly on his surroundings, can be stitched on a variety of gift items. When finished in a plastic magnet and placed on the refrigerator door, he'll serve as a gentle reminder to the midnight snacker. Of course, this pudgy character should only be given to those folks who are not actively dieting, or to those who possess a great sense of humor!

HE WHO INDULGES BULGES

	DMC	COLOR
3	white	white
I	415	pearl gray
x	318	steel gray, light
●	413	pewter gray, dark
o	3051	green-gray, dark
<	3052	green-gray, medium
–	335	rose
•	799	delft, medium
∪	729	old gold, medium

Fabric used for model: 14-count white Aida

Stitch count: 37H x 40W

Approximate design size:

14-count—2 ⅝" x 2 ⅞"

18-count—2 ¼" x 2 ⅜"

Instructions: Cross stitch using two strands of floss. Backstitch using one strand of floss. Make French knots for pig's nose using two strands 413, wrapping around needle twice.

Backstitch (bs) instructions:

413   pig

3051   letters and stems

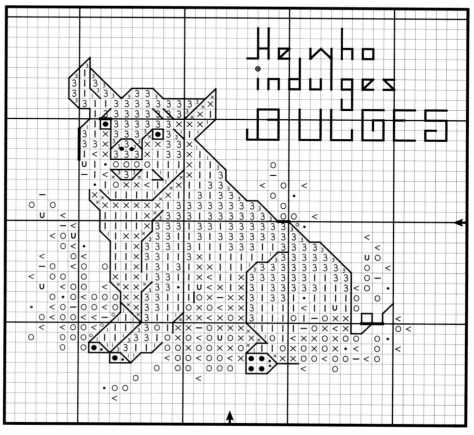

Gifts
To Mark This Day

Using finely stitched cross stitch pieces is an excellent way to mark important days in your life, and in the lives of those close to you. Every day can be a wonderful memory marked in stitches. Use the designs in this chapter to highlight traditional holidays, as well as life changing occasions such as retirement and graduation.

Welcome Little One

Stitching for children is always fun and when the resulting design is a delightful collection of wee farm animals, the pleasure is doubled. Using pre-finished items to stitch variations of this chart allows you to plan a nursery decor, or simply stitch a gift for the new baby!

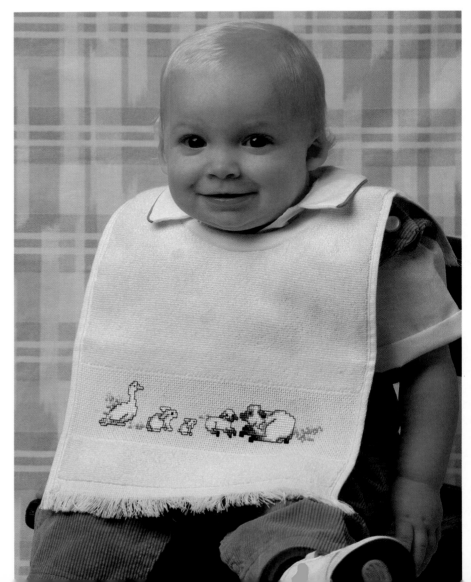

WELCOME LITTLE ONE

	DMC	COLOR
●	310	black
x	317	pewter gray
o	318	steel gray, light
c	415	pearl gray
•	white	white
7	776	pink, medium
∵	744	yellow, pale
∥	471	avocado green, very light
3	793	cornflower blue, medium
L	743	yellow, medium
+	3053	green-gray
z	3052	green-gray, medium

Fabric used for models: 14-count forget-me-not blue Aida from Wichelt Imports, Inc.; yellow bib from Charles Craft, Inc.
Stitch count: 46H x 111W
Approximate design size:
    14-count—3 ⅜" x 8"
    18-count—2 ⅝" x 6 ¼"

Instructions: Cross stitch using three strands of floss. Backstitch using one strand 310. Make French knots using one strand of floss, wrapping around needle twice.
French knots:
    310   ducks' eyes and bunnies' eyes
    776   bunny's nose

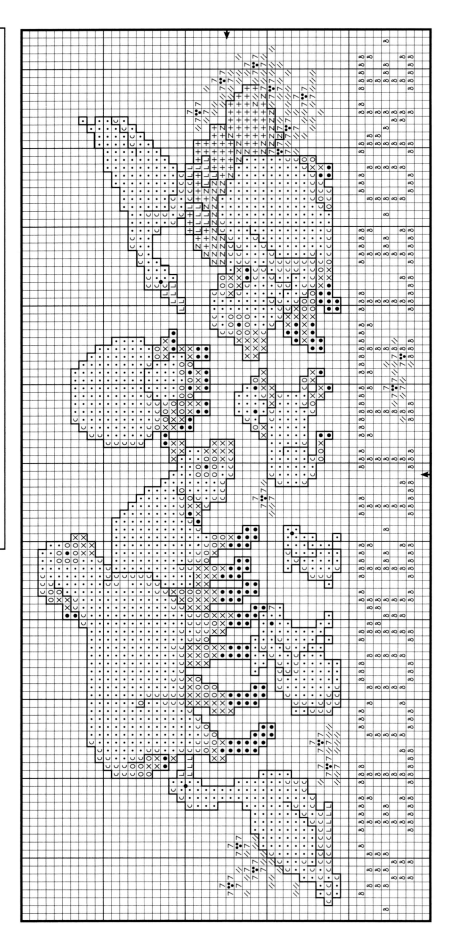

Mother's Day

Scattered pastel flowers surround a heart created by unstitched spaces on which the words "Mother's Day" are stitched. Meandering backstitches embellish the heart and are used to stitch the year.

MOTHER'S DAY

	DMC	COLOR
•	white	white
7	453	shell gray, light
c	818	baby pink
⁄⁄	776	pink, medium
∨	3326	rose, light
s	899	rose, medium
●	335	rose
M	309	rose, deep
:	828	blue, ultra light
∧	827	blue, very light
L	813	blue, light
z	826	blue, medium
⁄	211	lavender, light
‖	210	lavender, medium
J	209	lavender, dark
N	208	lavender, very dark
3	744	yellow, pale
x	743	yellow, medium
o	742	tangerine, light
T	725	topaz
H	783	Christmas gold
F	3347	yellow-green, medium
●	3346	hunter green
△	523	fern green, light
⅍	522	fern green
8	840	beige-brown, medium
R	838	beige-brown, very dark
2	702	kelly green

Fabric used for model: 18-count ivory Aida
Stitch count: 49H x 60W
Approximate design size:
    14-count—3 ½" x 4 ½"
    18-count—2 ¾" x 3 ½"

Instructions: Cross stitch using two strands of floss. Backstitch using one strand 826.

Baby Things

Any new mother will welcome useful baby gifts, and she'll be especially fond of those you stitch by hand. You can create a matched set from two separate pieces by repeating the design on both a bottle cover and the band of a hand towel. For variety, stitch your favorite on a bib, or on the chest pocket of a pair of bib overalls.

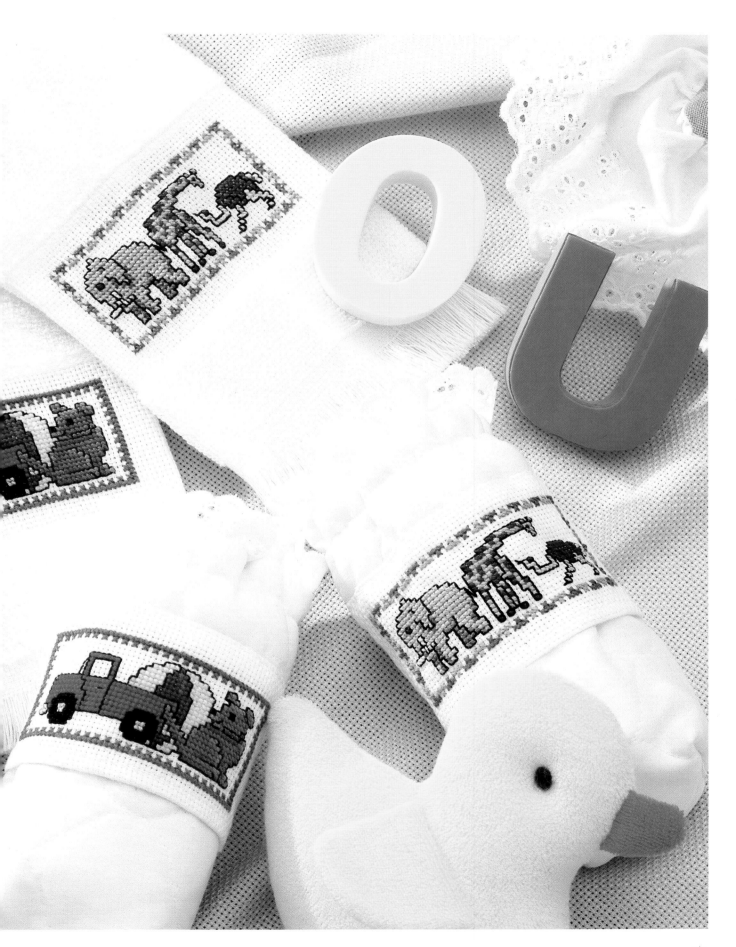

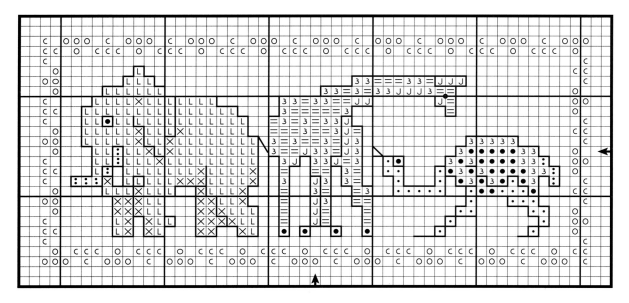

ANIMAL FAIR

	DMC	COLOR
L	648	beaver gray, light
x	646	beaver gray, dark
=	437	tan, light
3	801	coffee brown, dark
●	898	coffee brown, very dark
•	950	sportsman flesh, light
c	704	chartreuse, bright
o	701	Christmas green, light
:	ecru	ecru
J	436	tan
bs	310	black

Fabric used for models: 14-count white Aida bottle warmer from The Janlynn Corporation; 14-count white Park Avenue Fingertips™ towel from Charles Craft, Inc.
Stitch count: 23H x 53W
Approximate design size:
14-count—1 ⅝" x 3 ¾"
18-count—1 ¼" x 3"

Instructions: Cross stitch using three strands of floss. Backstitch using two strands 310. Make French knot for giraffe's eye using two strands 310, wrapping around needle twice.

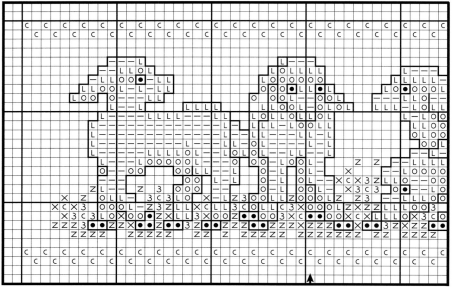

FOUR LAMBS

	DMC	COLOR
●	413	pewter gray, dark
o	415	pearl gray
L	762	pearl gray, very light
x	813	blue, light
3	3326	rose, light
c	745	yellow, light pale
z	3348	yellow-green, light
—	white	white
bs	414	steel gray, dark

Fabric used for models: 14-count white Aida bottle warmer from The Janlynn Corporation; 14-count white Aida Park Avenue Fingertips™ towel from Charles Craft, Inc.
Stitch count: 27H x width of item
Approximate design size:
14-count—2" x width of item

Instructions: Cross stitch using three strands of floss. Backstitch (bs) using two strands 414. **Note:** Stitch border to edges of towel and around bottle warmer.

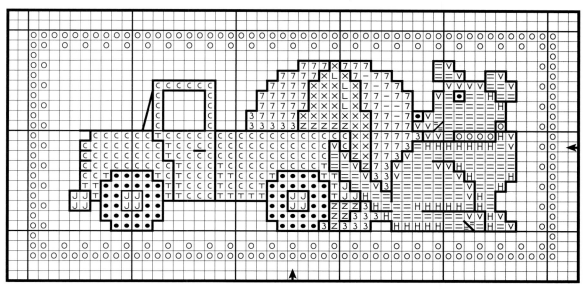

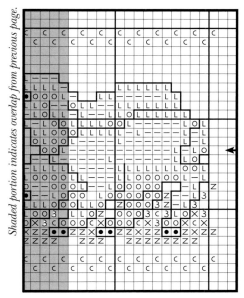

BOYS' TOYS

DMC	COLOR			
●	310	black	H 433	brown, medium
c	321	Christmas red	J 415	pearl gray
T	498	Christmas red, dark		
L	798	delft, dark		
x	797	royal blue		
z	796	royal blue, dark		
−	745	yellow, light pale		
7	744	yellow, pale		
3	743	yellow, medium		
o	701	Christmas green, light		
V	435	brown, very light		
=	434	brown, light		

Fabric used for models: 14-count white Aida bottle warmer from The Janlynn Corporation; 14-count white Aida Park Avenue Fingertips™ towel from Charles Craft, Inc.
Stitch count: 23H x 51W
Approximate design size:
    14-count—1 ⅝" x 3 ⅝"
    18-count—1 ¼" x 2 ⅞"

Instructions: Cross stitch using three strands of floss. Backstitch using two strands 310.

Treat Bags

This collection of ever-popular Halloween motifs is sure to bring smiles from all who see them! Finished as miniature treat bags and filled with goodies, they'll make ideal fright night decorations for a Halloween costume party, and you can award them as prizes to those sporting the best costumes. Of course, your favorite little ones who go bump in the night will like them, too!

TREAT BAGS

DMC	COLOR
⟍ 318	steel gray, light
x 844	beaver gray, ultra dark
c 553	violet, medium
y 725	topaz
V 720	orange spice, dark
z 721	orange spice, medium
• 722	orange spice, light
╱ 727	topaz, very light
+ white	white

Fabric used for models: 14-count white Aida

Bugsy
Stitch count: 32H x 30W
Approximate design size:
    14-count—2 ¼" x 2 ⅛"
    18-count—1 ¾" x 1 ⅝"

Great Pumpkin
Stitch count: 32H x 27W
Approximate design size:
    14-count—2 ¼" x 2"
    18-count—1 ¾" x 1 ½"

Boo Baby
Stitch count: 31H x 25W
Approximate design size:
    14-count—2 ¼" x 1 ⅞"
    18-count—1 ¾" x 1 ⅜"

The Ghostly Trio
Stitch count: 25H x 34W
Approximate design size:
    14-count—1 ⅞" x 2 ⅜"
    18-count—1 ⅜" x 1 ⅞"

Instructions: Cross stitch using two strands of floss. Backstitch using one strand of floss. Turn to page 140 for finishing instructions.

Backstitch (bs) instructions:
    317   all ghosts
    844   remainder of backstitching

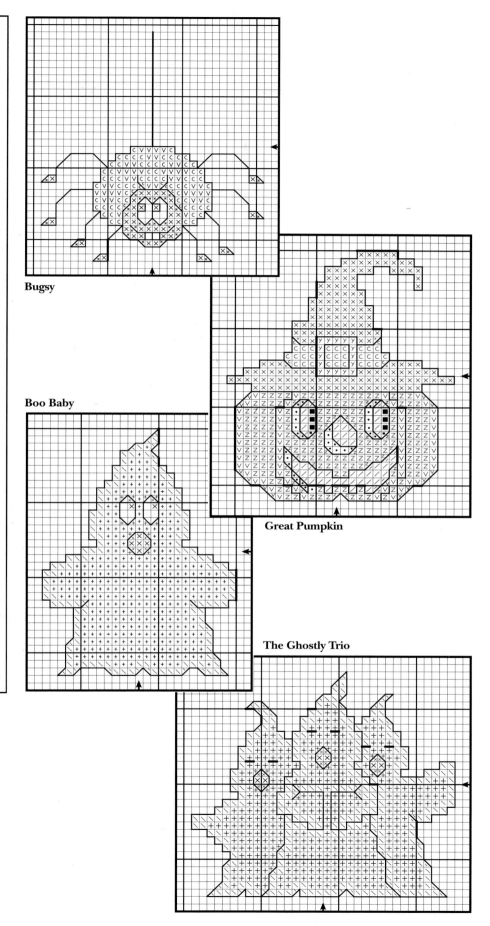

Bugsy

Boo Baby

Great Pumpkin

The Ghostly Trio

Woven Ribbon And Sweet Sixteen

Capture a young girl's heart with a gift she's sure to cherish for many years to come. A trinket box topped with your cross stitch will be an ideal gift for the young miss in your life. Muted shades of floss have been worked to create a woven-ribbon effect in the design atop the mauve trinket box, while a pastel garland of flowers and greenery, worked to form a heart around the lettering for *Sweet Sixteen*, completes the second design.

SWEET SIXTEEN

	DMC	COLOR
x	761	salmon, light
o	932	antique blue, light
L	503	blue-green, medium
V	502	blue-green
•	745	yellow, light pale
bs	3328	salmon, medium

Fabric used for model: 18-count white Aida
Stitch count: 41H x 38W
Approximate design size:
   14-count—3" x 2 ¾"
   18-count—2 ¼" x 2 ⅛"

Instructions: Cross stitch using two strands of floss. Backstitch using one strand of floss.
Backstitch (bs) instructions:
•••• 503   — 3328

WOVEN RIBBON

	DMC	COLOR
c	3689	mauve, light
o	3688	mauve, medium
3	3687	mauve
L	369	pistachio green, very light
=	368	pistachio green, light
z	320	pistachio green, medium
●	319	pistachio green, very dark

Fabric used for model: 18-count white Aida

Stitch count: 47H x 44W

Approximate design size:
    14-count—3 ⅜" x 3 ⅛"
    18-count—2 ⅝" x 2 ⅜"

Instructions: Cross stitch using two strands of floss.

Happy Birthday!

Add to the joy of festive birthday celebrations by stitching a place setting
designated for the birthday person.
Just a few quick passes of your needle
will transform an ordinary napkin
and place mat into an extraordinary
place of honor for the lucky cel-
ebrant. Bright, cheery stitchery colors will add to the festive mood of the
occasion! Stitch this set for your child's
birthday, or present to a friend on
her happy day.

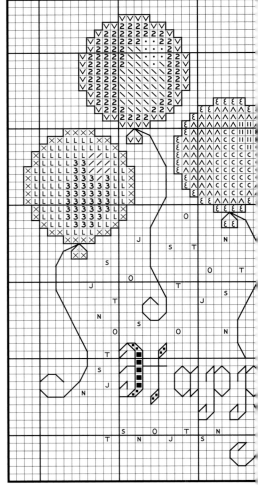

HAPPY BIRTHDAY!

DMC	COLOR
s 210	lavender, medium
T 352	coral, light
o 518	wedgewood, light
x 600	cranberry, very dark
L 602	cranberry, medium
3 604	cranberry, light
⁄ 605	cranberry, very light
N 743	yellow, medium
V 796	royal blue, dark
2 798	delft, dark
\ 799	delft, medium
• 809	delft
ε 909	emerald green, very dark
∧ 911	emerald green, medium
c 912	emerald green, light
‖ 913	nile green, medium
J 956	geranium
■ 601	cranberry, dark
bs 3371	black-brown

Fabric used for model: 27-count white Super Linen from Charles Craft, Inc.
Stitch count: 59H x 87W (full design)
Approximate design size:
  14-count—4 ¼" x 6 ¼"
  18-count—3 ⅜" x 4 ⅞"
  27-count—4 ⅜" x 6 ⅜"

Stitch count: 32H x 15W (balloon)

Approximate design size:
  14-count—2 ⅜" x 1 ⅛"
  18-count—1 ⅞" x ⅞"
  27-count—2 ⅞" x 1 ⅛"

Instructions: Cross stitch using two strands of floss. Backstitch using two strands of floss. Turn to page 140 for finishing instructions. **Note:** Dimensions for a standard size place mat (13" x 18") and napkin (15" x 15"). Design stitched on napkin is first balloon of large design.
Backstitch (bs) instructions:
  3371   balloons and string
  601   lettering

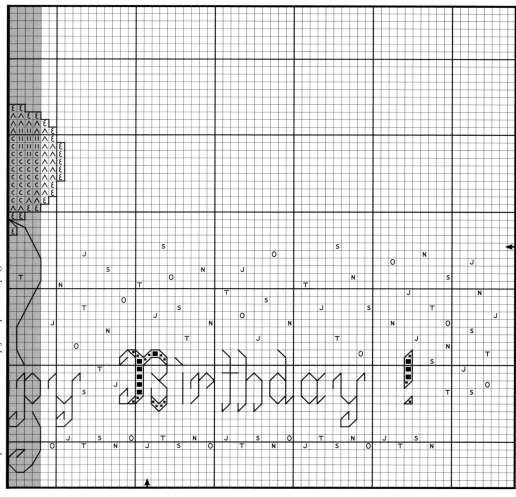

Shaded portion indicates overlap from previous page.

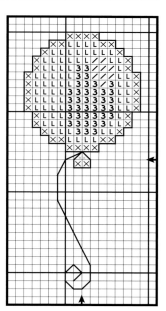

Celebrate In Style

Surprise your love on St. Valentine's Day with a delectable meal you have prepared and serve it in romantic surroundings. Whether your mood calls for a Victorian party setting, a picnic spread by the fireplace, or a candlelit dinner at the kitchen table, place mats and napkins you have stitched will add to the romance of the occasion.

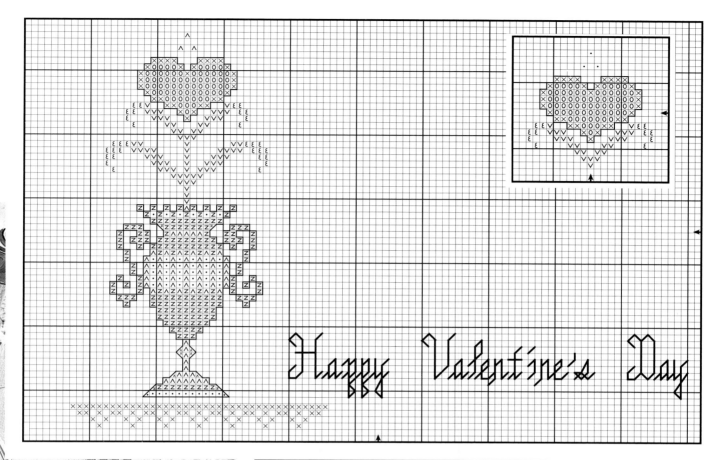

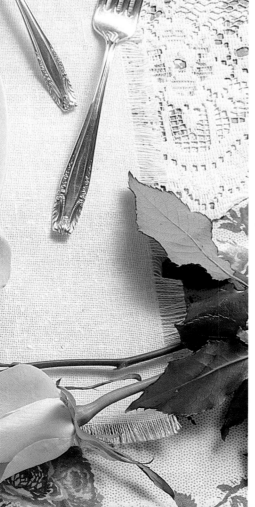

CELEBRATE IN STYLE

	DMC	COLOR
x	309	rose, deep
o	899	rose, medium
V	501	blue-green, dark
ε	500	blue-green, very dark
z	3042	antique violet, light
∧	3041	antique violet, medium
•	3326	rose, light
bs	3371	black-brown

Fabric used for model: 27-count white Super Linen from Charles Craft, Inc.
Stitch count: 62H x 93W (full design)
Approximate design size:
  14-count—4 ½" x 6 ⅝"
  18-count—3 ½" x 3 ¼"
  27-count—4 ⅝" x 6 ⅞"

Stitch count: 18H x 19W (napkin)
Approximate design size:
  14-count—1 ⅜" x 1 ⅜"
  18-count—1" x 1 ⅛"
  27-count—1 ¼" x 1 ⅜"

Instructions: Cross stitch over two threads using two strands of floss. Backstitch using one strand of floss. Turn to page 140 for finishing instructions. **Note:** Dimensions for a standard size place mat (13" x 18") and napkin (15" x 15").
Backstitch (bs) instructions:
  309   lettering
  3371 heart and vase

Thee I Love

Reaffirm the wonder of newly found love with this stitchery which is just right for an anniversary celebration. Clusters of fragrant lily of the valley bells coupled with loving words make a lasting memento of your wedding day. Convey your message with this tasteful treasure.

THEE I LOVE

DMC	COLOR
● 319	pistachio green, very dark
x 367	pistachio green, dark
c 320	pistachio green, medium
V 368	pistachio green, light
= 369	pistachio green, very light
o white	white
+ 415	pearl gray
3 745	yellow, light pale
∕ 368	pistachio green, light (half cross)
bs 890	pistachio green, ultra dark
bs 317	pewter gray

Fabric used for model: 25-count moss green Lugana® from Zweigart®
Stitch count: 67H x 98W
Approximate design size:
14-count—4 ¾" x 7"
18-count—3 ¾" x 5 ½"
25-count—5 ⅜" x 7 ⅞"

Instructions: Cross stitch over two threads using two strands of floss. Backstitch using one strand of floss unless otherwise indicated.
Backstitch (bs) instructions:
317   flowers
319   tip of bottom left leaf, bottom edge of lower right

leaf, lower left side and tip of large background leaf
320   bottom left leaf **except** tip, upper left side to tip of large background leaf, bottom right edge and left side of large center leaf to tip
368   top of lower right leaf, right side of large background leaf
369   center line in large center leaf
890   flower stems, lettering and border (two strands)

Father's Day Duo

This pair of mirror-image cross stitched ducks will add the finishing, masculine touch to the study or den of that special man in your life. If he's a hunter, he may opt to hang this pair in his trophy room. Great for Father's Day!

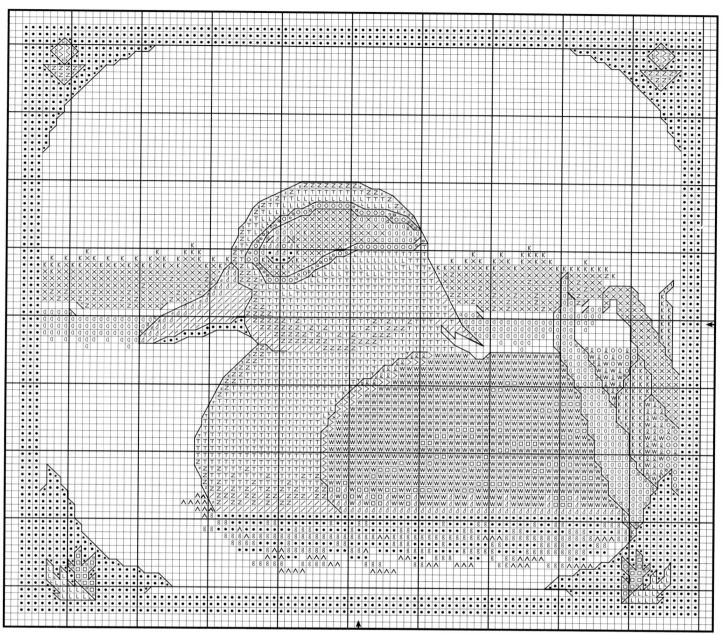

**GREEN WINGED TEAL
(LEFT AND RIGHT)**

DMC	COLOR
● 336	navy blue
8 322	navy, very light
∧ 775	baby blue, light
o 762	pearl gray, very light
∕ 3031	mocha brown, very dark
> 420	hazelnut brown, dark
ℓ 452	shell gray, medium
∂ 610	drab brown, very dark
x 937	avocado green, medium
◁ 935	avocado green, dark
K 731	olive green, dark
L 301	mahogany, medium

z 300	mahogany, very dark
T 918	red-copper, dark
w 869	hazelnut brown, very dark
□ 725	topaz

Fabric used for model: 14-count Fiddler's
Lite from Charles Craft, Inc.
Stitch count: 87H x 97W
Approximate design size:
   14-count—6 ¼" x 7"
   18-count—4 ⅞" x 5 ⅜"

Instructions: Cross stitch using two strands
of floss. Backstitch using one strand of floss.
Backstitch (bs) instructions:
   610   duck's bill

762	band around to back of
	head, duck's eye, lower half
	of duck's eye
869	duck's head and back
918	duck's breast
420	duck's shoulder
935	leaf containing symbol ◁
937	leaf containing symbol z,
	corner decoration
	containing symbol z
420	corner decoration
	containing symbol >
301	corner decoration
	containing symbol L
725	corner decoration
	containing symbol □

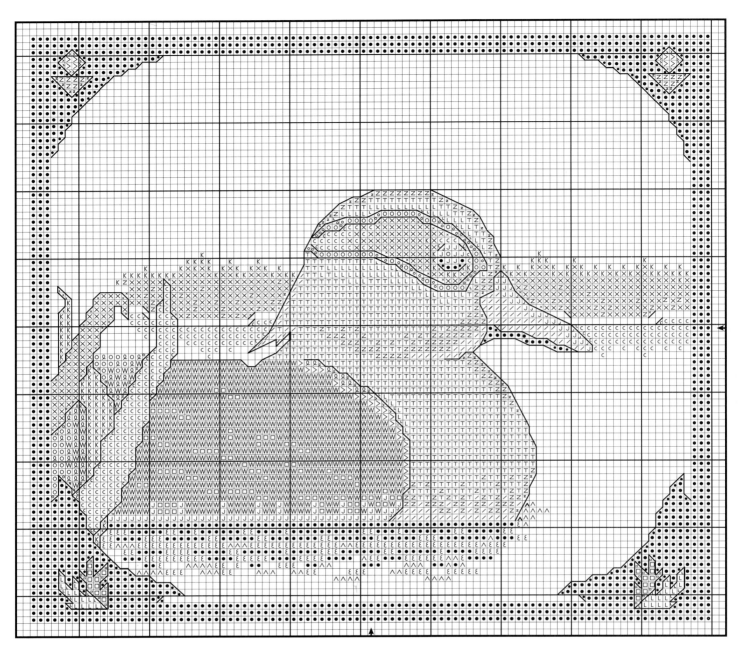

GREEN WINGED TEAL
(LEFT AND RIGHT)

	DMC	COLOR
●	336	navy blue
ε	322	navy, very light
∧	775	baby blue, light
o	762	pearl gray, very light
╱	3031	mocha brown, very dark
>	420	hazelnut brown, dark
ℓ	452	shell gray, medium
J	610	drab brown, very dark
x	937	avocado green, medium
c	935	avocado green, dark
K	731	olive green, dark
L	301	mahogany, medium

z	300	mahogany, very dark
T	918	red-copper, dark
w	869	hazelnut brown, very dark
□	725	topaz

Fabric used for model: 14-count Fiddler's
Lite from Charles Craft, Inc.
Stitch count: 87H x 97W
Approximate design size:
    14-count—6 ¼" x 7"
    18-count—4 ⅞" x 5 ⅜"

Instructions: Cross stitch using two strands
of floss. Backstitch using one strand of floss.
Backstitch (bs) instructions:
    610   duck's bill

762	band around to back of head, duck's eye, lower half of duck's eye
869	duck's head and back
918	duck's breast
420	duck's shoulder
935	leaf containing symbol c
937	leaf containing symbol z, corner decoration containing symbol z
420	corner decoration containing symbol >
301	corner decoration containing symbol L
725	corner decoration containing symbol □

Graduation Day

Honor your favorite graduate as she celebrates the day marking culmination of twelve years of education! The design, with an original verse, could be used as a salute to a college graduate as well. An alphabet is included for personalizing your work.

Since you've been in school,
It's been nothing but a hassel.
But now you're a graduate,
Be proud of that tassel!
Always believe in yourself,
Traveling the road to success.
By working hard today,
Tomorrow you'll be the best!

CATHERINE COCKERHAM
ASHBROOK HIGH SCHOOL
JUNE 1, 1990
DIPLOMA WITH HONORS

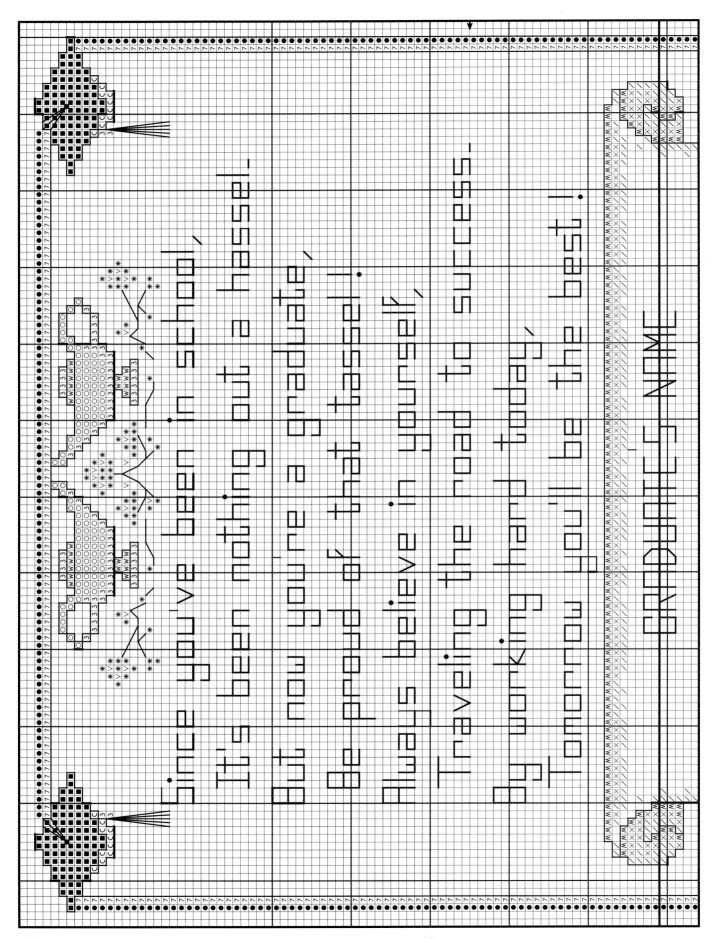

Since you've been in school,

It's been nothing but a hassel.

But now you're a graduate,

Be proud of that tassel!

Always believe in yourself,

Traveling the road to success.

By working hard today,

Tomorrow you'll be the best!

GRADUATE'S NAME

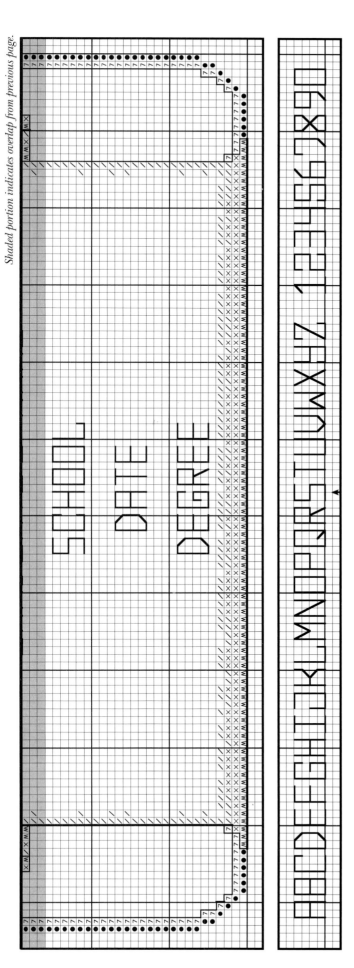

GRADUATION DAY

	DMC	COLOR
c	414	steel gray, dark
■	310	black
w	780	topaz, very dark
3	782	topaz, medium
o	783	Christmas gold
*	319	pistachio green, very dark
V	367	pistachio green, dark
M	318	steel gray, light
x	415	pearl gray
⁄	762	pearl gray, very light
●		See **Note** below
7		See **Note** below
bs	3371	black-brown

Fabric used for model: 14-count white Aida
Stitch count: 110H x 114W
Approximate design size:
14-count—7 ⅞" x 8 ⅛"
18-count—6 ⅛" x 6 ¼"

Instructions: Cross stitch using two strands of floss. Backstitch using one strand of floss unless indicated otherwise. Straight stitch tassel and tassel cord over edge of cap using one strand each of school colors. Make French knots for center of each cap using two strands of floss, wrapping around needle twice. **Note:** Choose color to match darkest school color for symbol ●; choose color to match lightest school color for symbol 7. Use alphabet to personalize.
Backstitch (bs) instructions:

414 scroll
310 caps
3371 poem (two strands), lamps, ivy vines
darkest school color–border's inside edges-sides/top
choice of school colors for name, school, date, and degree (two strands)

Poem by Cathy Livingston

Happy Hanukkah

Please your friends who observe this Jewish holiday by stitching for them an elegant design to mark the season. A menorah with red candles forms the central motif with a Magen David in the center. *Happy Hanukkah* spelled out in stitched letters completes the design.

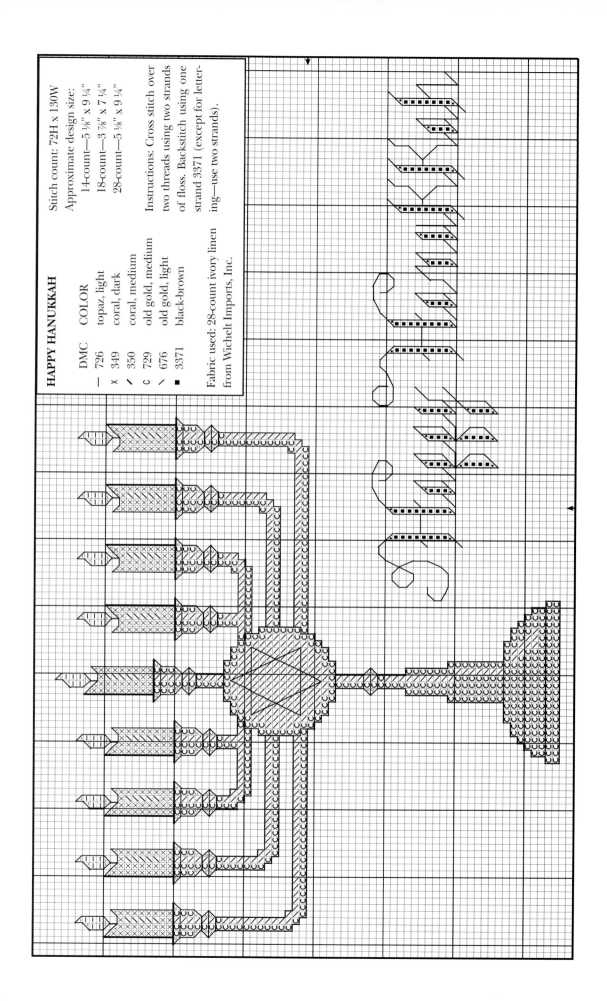

HAPPY HANUKKAH

Stitch count: 72H x 130W

Approximate design size:
14-count—5⅛" x 9¼"
18-count—3⅞" x 7¼"
28-count—5⅛" x 9¼"

DMC		COLOR
—	726	topaz, light
x	349	coral, dark
↘	350	coral, medium
c	729	old gold, medium
↘	676	old gold, light
■	3371	black-brown

Instructions: Cross stitch over two threads using two strands of floss. Backstitch using one strand 3371 (except for lettering—use two strands).

Fabric used: 28-count ivory linen from Wichelt Imports, Inc.

Celebrate Retirement!

Ah, the retired life! A suitable gift for the one who has recently retired, this piece paints the picture of leisure. Surprise a recently retired parent, mate, or friend with this unique gift, or package the materials and suggest that they use new-found free time to stitch it!

CELEBRATE RETIREMENT!

	DMC	COLOR
▲	938	coffee, ultra dark
●	801	coffee, dark
╱	726	topaz, light
⫽	3078	golden yellow, very light
·	3753	antique blue, ultra very light
o	950	flesh, light
−	948	peach flesh, very light
■	311	navy, medium
w	312	navy, light
z	349	coral, dark
c	350	coral, medium
3	986	forest, very dark
V	987	forest, dark
L	989	forest
x	371	mustard
╲	372	mustard, light
∪	322	navy, very light
bs	3371	black-brown

Fabric used for model: 14-count white Aida
Stitch count: 84H x 60W
Approximate design size:
    14-count—6" x 4 ⅜"
    18-count—4 ⅝" x 3 ⅜"

Instructions: Cross stitch using two strands of floss. Backstitch using one strand of floss unless indicated otherwise. Straight stitch (ss) using one strand of floss.
Backstitch (bs) instructions:
    312   shoe straps
    349   name (two strands)
    3371   lettering (two strands)
    726   sun's inside edge
    3371   remainder of backstitching

Straight stitch (ss):
    726   sun's rays
    987   grass blades

Gifts For Christmas

Holiday stitchery is a natural! Many avid stitchers work all year on delightful projects to present at Christmastime to friends and relatives. Within this chapter, you'll find a collection of the very best Christmas designs which will be used year after year with great pride!

Christmas Village

Christmas Village, shown here, brings the holiday spirit to the dining table with quaint place mats stitched in silhouette fashion. Use your imagination and this chart to also create napkins, towel borders, ornaments, and a lovely framed village scene.

CHRISTMAS VILLAGE

DMC	COLOR
z white	white (blue place mat)
z 930	antique blue, dark (white place mat)

Fabric used for models: 14-count colonial blue place mat and 14-count white place mat from Craft World®, Inc.

Stitch count for Santa's sleigh: 25H x 25W
Stitch count for trees: 25H x 57W
Stitch count for houses: 25H x 139W

Instructions: Cross stitch using three strands of floss.

Each design is stitched starting two threads in from woven border on place mat and napkin.

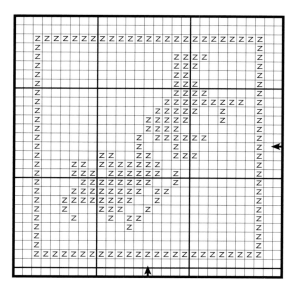

Shaded portion indicates overlap.

Peace On Earth Sampler

This twentieth-century sampler, with its message of peace, is designed to hang in your home during the Christmas season, and all year if you so choose. Various parts of the chart can be stitched separately and finished as ornaments, smaller framed pieces, or bookmarks. Because of its traditional styling, the sampler would be equally at home in a log cabin or on the wall of a high-rise apartment. Why not stitch two—one for your home and one for the person who taught you to stitch!

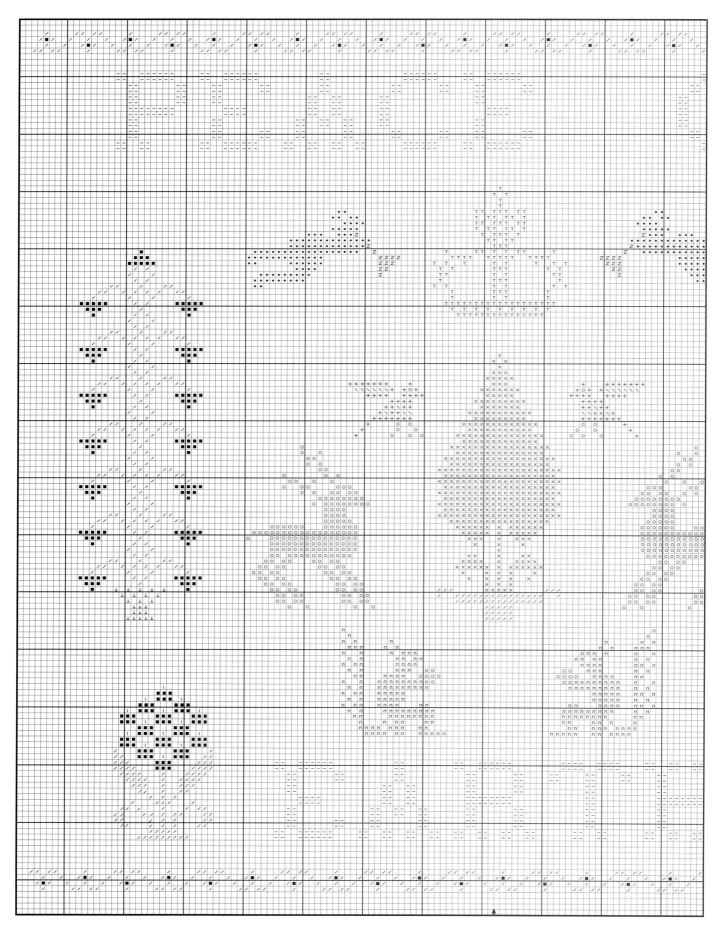

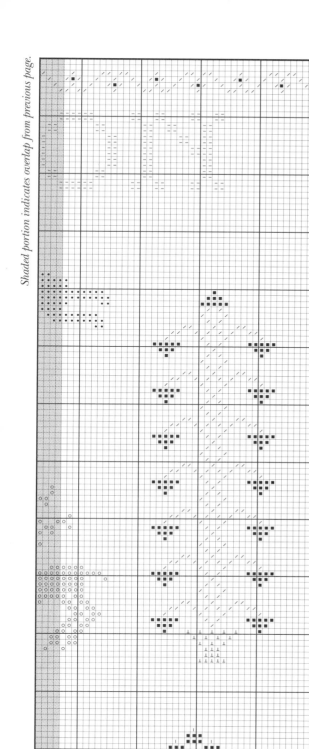

PEACE ON EARTH SAMPLER

	DMC	COLOR
■	347	salmon, dark
z	422	hazelnut brown, light
o	3021	brown-gray, dark
⊓	610	drab brown, very dark
⁄	3345	hunter green
x	895	Christmas green, dark
–	816	garnet
+	926	gray-green, dark
⧵	930	antique blue, dark
•	822	beige-gray, light
T	739	tan, ultra light
⊥	801	coffee brown, dark
I	948	peach flesh, very light

Fabric used for models: 14-count summer khaki Aida and 14-count cream Aida
Stitch count: 150H x 154W (complete design)
Approximate design size:
   14-count—10 ¾" x 11"
   18-count—8 ⅜" x 8 ⅝"

Instructions: Cross stitch using two strands of floss. Turn to pages 140 and 141 for finishing instructions. **Note:** Also shown are different ways motifs can be used to create other designs.

Merry Christmas

Give a gift sure to please—a holiday greeting designed for display in a foyer, entry hall, or sitting room. The bold *Merry Christmas*, surrounded by a flurry of holiday bells, is enhanced by the custom-cut mat. Newlyweds will enjoy this personalized picture and will display it proudly each Christmas.

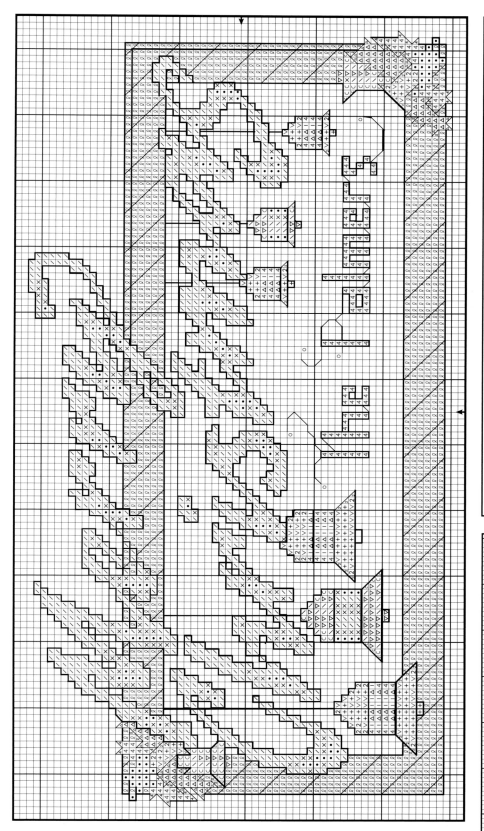

MERRY CHRISTMAS

	DMC	COLOR
⁄	335	rose
x	321	Christmas red
•	815	garnet, medium
△	704	chartreuse, bright
I	702	kelly green
4	700	Christmas green, bright
▽	762	pearl gray, very light
＼	318	steel gray, light
c	317	pewter gray
+	727	topaz, very light
V	725	topaz
2	782	topaz, medium
ℓ	3348	yellow-green, light
o	895	Christmas green, dark
bs	902	garnet, very dark
bs	310	black

Fabric used for model: 32-count white
Belfast linen from Zweigart®
Stitch count: 62H x 116W
Approximate design size:
    14-count—4 ½" x 8 ⅝"
    18-count—3 ½" x 6 ½"
    32-count—3 ⅞" x 7 ¼"

Instructions: Cross stitch over two threads
using two strands of floss. Backstitch (bs)
using one strand of floss.
Backstitch instructions:
    902 *Merry Christmas*, border
           stripes, border outline
    895 name, line inside green border
    310 remainder of backstitching

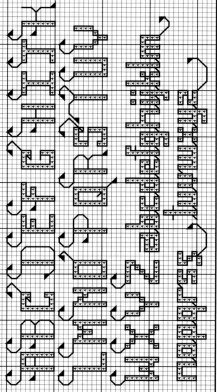

TOP

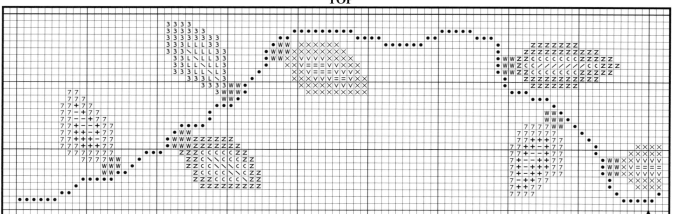

Holiday Lights

Looking for a very impressive gift that can be finished in record time? Use ready-to-stitch place mats and add your finishing touch with this bright string of holiday tree lights. These make a clever hostess gift when the occasion calls for something wonderful!

HOLIDAY LIGHTS

	DMC	COLOR
x	817	coral red, very dark
V	349	coral, dark
=	350	coral, medium
7	824	blue, very dark
+	825	blue, dark
−	826	blue, medium
z	699	Christmas green
c	700	Christmas green, bright
∕	702	kelly green
3	725	topaz
L	726	topaz, light
∖	727	topaz, very light
●	890	pistachio green, ultra dark
w	319	pistachio green, very dark

Fabric used for model: 18-count white Aida on red/white place mat from Tish & Amy Originals
Stitch count: 26H x 180W
Approximate design size:
    18-count—1½" x 10"

Instructions: Cross stitch using two strands of floss.

TOP

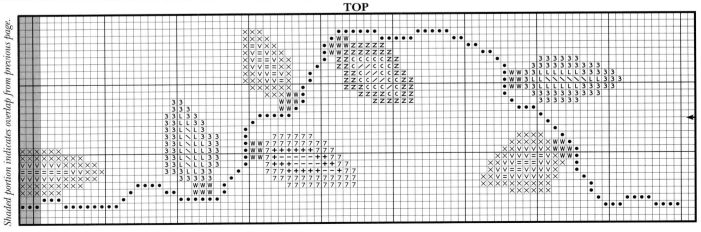

Shaded portion indicates overlap from previous page.

Christmas Animal Wreath

With three simple country critters, a paper teddy garland, a bow, and a small grapevine wreath, you can quickly assemble this attractive addition to someone's holiday decor. For a larger wreath, stitch additional critters, or stitch several using only one design and create a theme wreath for a friend to use on a wall or protected door.

CHRISTMAS ANIMAL WREATH

	DMC	COLOR
<	221	shell pink, dark
o	223	shell pink, medium
●	415	pearl gray
x	500	blue-green, very dark
I	501	blue-green, dark
z	729	old gold, medium
•	white	white
bs	413	pewter gray, dark

Fabric used for model: 14-count white Aida
Stitch count: 31H x 31W
Approximate design size:
    14-count—2 ¼" x 2 ¼"
    18-count—1 ¾" x 1 ¾"

Instructions: Cross stitch using two strands of floss. Backstitch animals using one strand 413. Make French knots for eyes and pig's nose using one strand 413, wrapping around needle twice. Turn to page 140 for finishing instructions.

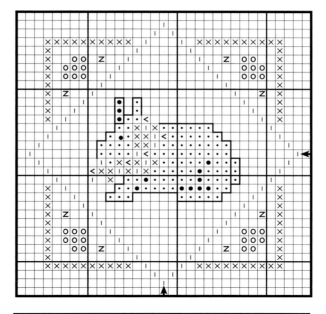

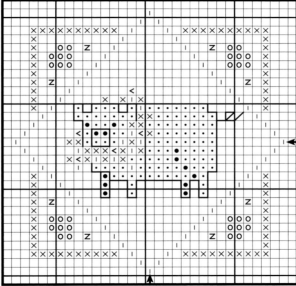

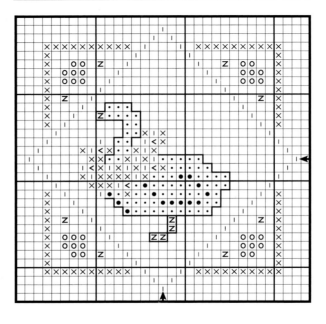

First Christmas

Everyone loves to recall those special "first" occasions in their lives, and this trio of designs for a first Christmas will trigger many fond memories for newlyweds, first-time grandparents, and baby's family. Framed as shown, or made into small pillows, these designs will be welcomed as your stitched salute to those first celebrations.

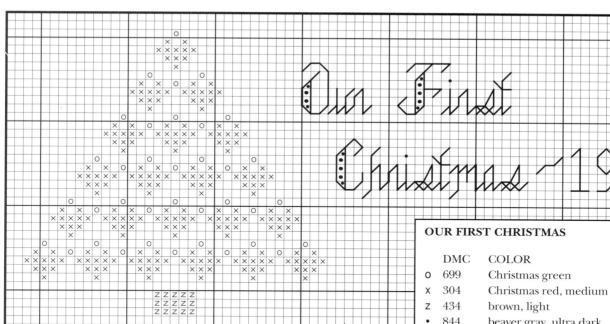

OUR FIRST CHRISTMAS

	DMC	COLOR
o	699	Christmas green
x	304	Christmas red, medium
z	434	brown, light
•	844	beaver gray, ultra dark

Fabric used for model: 27-count white linen from Wichelt Imports, Inc.
Stitch count: 34H x 74W
Approximate design size:
    14-count—2 ⅜" x 5 ¼"
    18-count—1 ⅞" x 4 ⅛"
    27-count—2 ½" x 5 ½"

Instructions: Cross stitch over two threads using two strands of floss. Backstitch using one strand 844.

GRANDPARENTS' FIRST CHRISTMAS

	DMC	COLOR
x	666	red, bright
•	321	red
o	738	tan, very light
\	701	green, light
z	435	brown, very light
/	436	tan
>	987	forest, dark
c	304	red, medium
••	973	canary, bright
■	3371	black-brown
bs	844	beaver gray, ultra dark

Fabric used for model: 27-count white linen from Wichelt Imports, Inc.
Stitch count: 46H x 61W
Approximate design size:
    14-count—3 ¼" x 4 ⅜"
    18-count—2 ½" x 3 ⅜"
    27-count—3 ⅜" x 4 ½"

Instructions: Cross stitch over two threads using two strands of floss. Backstitch using one strand of floss.
Backstitch (bs) instructions:
    304   lettering
    3371   eyes, nose, and mouth
    844   remainder of backstitching

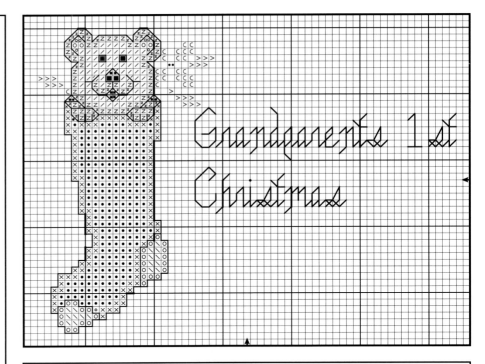

BABY'S FIRST CHRISTMAS

	DMC	COLOR
x	435	brown, very light
\	738	tan, very light
/	436	tan
■	3371	black-brown
•	437	tan, light
o	321	Christmas red
z	700	Christmas green, bright

Fabric used for model: 27-count white linen from Wichelt Imports, Inc.

Stitch count: 34H x 67W
Approximate design size:
    14-count—2 ⅜" x 4 ¾"
    18-count—1 ⅞" x 3 ¾"
    27-count—2 ½" x 5"

Instructions: Cross stitch over two threads using two strands of floss. Backstitch using one strand of floss unless indicated otherwise.
Backstitch (bs) instructions:
    321   lettering (two strands)
    3371   eyes, nose, mouth
    844   remainder of backstitching

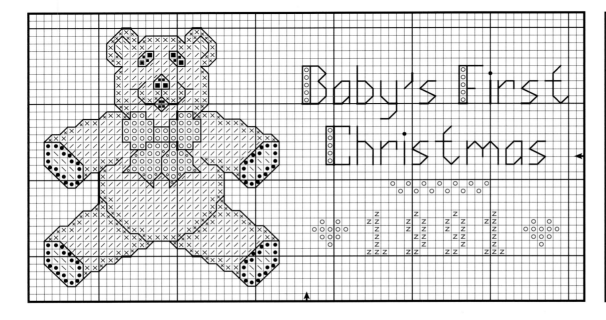

Holly Motif

If your time is limited and your gift list is long, use your spare moments to add a festive touch to towels you'll present as gifts. Color-coded for bright Christmas colors and for muted colors, these motifs also work well on place mats and napkins. A fingertip towel sporting this seasonal favorite will make an excellent stitch ahead, wrap ahead, and ready to go gift for teachers!

HOLLY MOTIF

	DMC	COLOR—BRIGHT
:	703	chartreuse
⁄	702	kelly green
•	701	Christmas green, light
x	321	Christmas red
bs	699	Christmas green

	DMC	COLOR—MUTED
:	523	fern green, light
⁄	522	fern green
•	3363	pine green, medium

x	498	Christmas red, dark
bs	520	fern green, dark

Fabric used for model: 14-count white Park Avenue Fingertips™ towel from Charles Craft, Inc.

Stitch count—Large: 25H x 68W
Approximate design size:
    14-count—1 ⅞" x 4 ⅞"
    18-count—1 ½" x 3 ⅞"
Stitch count—Small: 13H x 42W
Approximate design size:
    11-count—1 ¼" x 3 ⅞"

    14-count—1" x 3"
    18-count—¾" x 2 ⅜"
    22-count—⅝" x 2"

Instructions: Cross stitch using two strands of floss. Backstitch using one strand of floss.
Backstitch (bs) instructions:

498	berries (both color codes)
699	remainder of backstitching (bright color code)
520	remainder of backstitching (muted color code)

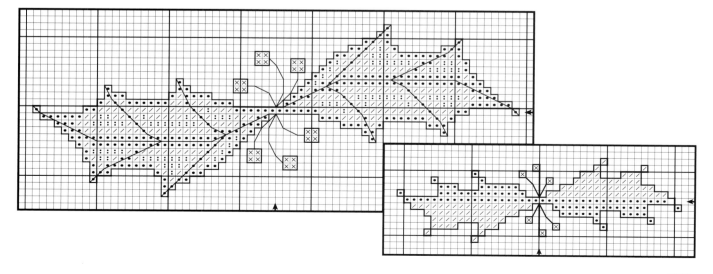

Gifts
To Share

If giving gifts from your kitchen has
appeal for you, dress up those goodies with another gift from your
hand—a cross stitched jar lid cover.
Introduce your famous jams and jellies with these quick fruit designs. Fill
small jars with hot chocolate mix, top
with the *Happy Holidays* design, and
present them to friends, teachers, the
mailman, anyone and everyone!
When the jam or hot chocolate mix is
gone, these make wonderful candy jars.

HAPPY HOLIDAYS

DMC   BALGER® COLOR

o	321		Christmas red
∕	367		pistachio, dark
v	319		pistachio, very dark
x		002	gold

Fabric used for model: 14-count white
Aida
Stitch count: 45H x 45W
Approximate design size:
      14-count—3 ¼" x 3 ¼"
      18-count—2 ½" x 2 ½"

Instructions: Cross stitch using two
strands of floss. Backstitch lettering using one strand 319. Turn to page 140
for finishing instructions.

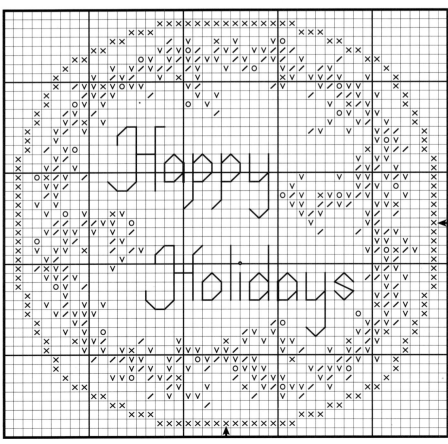

128

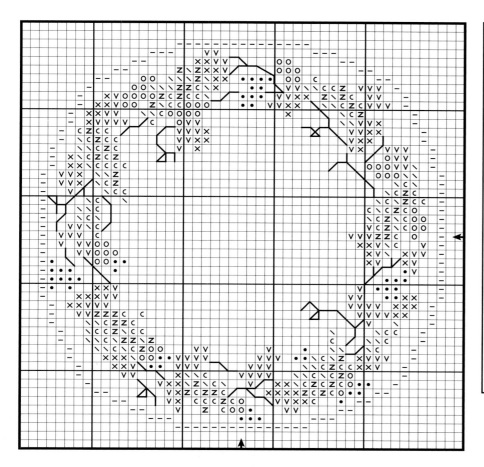

GRAPES

	DMC	COLOR
z	550	violet, very dark
c	553	violet, medium
\	554	violet, light
x	3011	khaki green, dark
V	3012	khaki green, medium
o	3362	pine green, dark
•	3363	pine green, medium
—	869	hazelnut brown, very dark

Fabric used for model: 14-count white Aida

Stitch count: 45H x 45W

Approximate design size:
    14-count—3 ¼" x 3 ¼"
    18-count—2 ½" x 2 ½"

Instructions: Cross stitch using two strands of floss. Backstitch vine using one strand 869. Turn to page 140 for finishing instructions.

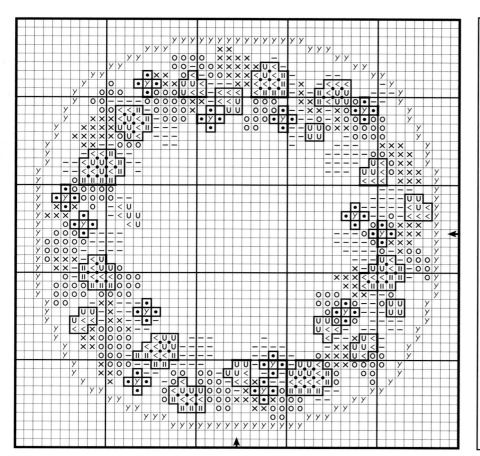

STRAWBERRIES

	DMC	COLOR
•	white	white
y	726	topaz, light
x	3345	hunter green, dark
—	3347	yellow-green, medium
o	3348	yellow-green, light
‖	816	garnet
<	347	salmon, dark
∪	3328	salmon, medium
bs	610	drab brown, very dark

Fabric used for model: 14-count white Aida

Stitch count: 45H x 45W

Approximate design size:
    14-count—3 ¼" x 3 ¼"
    18-count—2 ½" x 2 ½"

Instructions: Cross stitch using two strands of floss. Backstitch using one strand of floss. Turn to page 140 for finishing instructions.

Backstitch (bs) instructions:
    816   berries
    610   flowers

Christmas
And Welcome
Coasters

Friends who entertain will be delighted when they unwrap these cross stitch coasters, which are practical as well as pretty. Stitch the country-inspired welcome design for the friend who prefers a taste of the rural life, and the Christmas design for holiday get-togethers.

CHRISTMAS AND WELCOME COASTERS

DMC	COLOR
Christmas (country colors)	
x 986	forest, very dark
z 304	red, medium
> 433	brown, medium
Christmas (Victorian colors)	
> 640	beige-gray, very dark
x 502	blue-green
z 223	pink, medium
Welcome	
x 930	antique blue, dark
∕ 932	antique blue, light
3 640	beige-gray, very dark
z 221	pink, dark
7 223	pink, medium

Fabric used for model: Christmas: 27-count natural brown and cream linen from Norden Crafts; Welcome: 27-count natural brown linen from Norden Crafts

Stitch count: Christmas: 57H x 57W
        Welcome: 55H x 55W

Approximate design size (Christmas):
        14-count—4" x 4"
        18-count—3 ¼" x 3 ¼"
        27-count—4 ¼" x 4 ¼"

Approximate design size (Welcome):
        14-count—4" x 4"
        18-count—3" x 3"
        27-count—4 ⅛" x 4 ⅛"

Instructions: Cross stitch over two threads using two strands of floss. Backstitch using two strands of floss.

Backstitch (bs) instructions:
Christmas (country colors)
∿∿ 986   — 304
Christmas (Victorian colors)
∿∿ 502   — 223
Welcome
— 640   ···· 221   ∿∿ 930

Another gift idea: Stitch extra coaster and place in the lid of a box from Wheatland Crafts. Place finished coaster set in box–an attractive way to store your coasters. Turn to page 140 for finishing instructions.

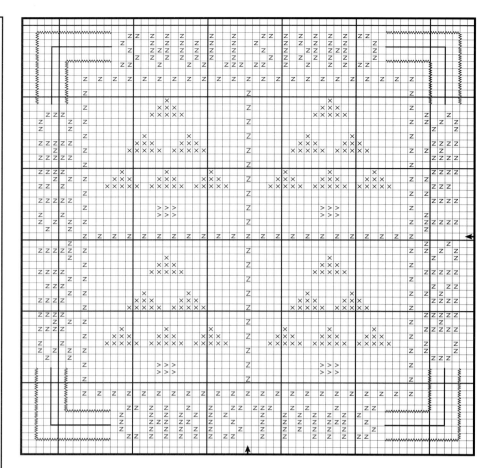

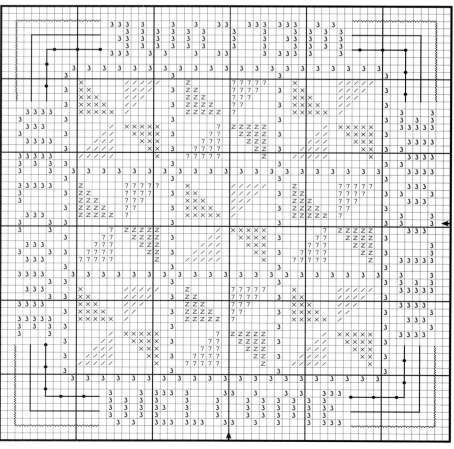

Noel

A holiday wreath, complete with a large red bow, forms one letter of the greeting in this simple design. Worked in traditional holiday colors of red and green, this simple greeting will be a welcome addition to a collection of favorite holiday decorations. Vary the fabric to best suit the decorating preference of the recipient. Use rustic colors and weaves to achieve a country look, or dress it up on clean linen. The floss colors work well on either.

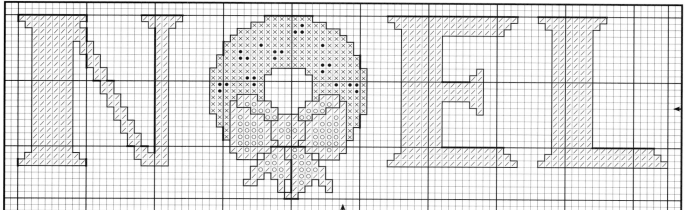

NOEL		
DMC	**COLOR**	
/ 304	Christmas red, medium	
o 321	Christmas red	
● 666	Christmas red, bright	
x 987	forest green, dark	
bs 645	beaver gray, very dark	

Fabric used for model: 27-count natural

Super Linen from Charles Craft, Inc.
Stitch count: 28H x 95W
Approximate design size:
   14-count—2" x 6 ¾"
   18-count—1 ½" x 5 ¼"
   27-count—2 ⅛" x 7"

Instructions: Cross stitch over two threads using two strands of floss. Backstitch using one strand 645.

Just Make Mine An Old-Fashioned Christmas

Framed for display, this piece is suitable for the one who loves the Christmases of yesteryear. Whether she displays it prominently on a wall or rests it in a tabletop easel in a welcoming foyer, this is a gift she's sure to use in decorating her home, season after holiday season.

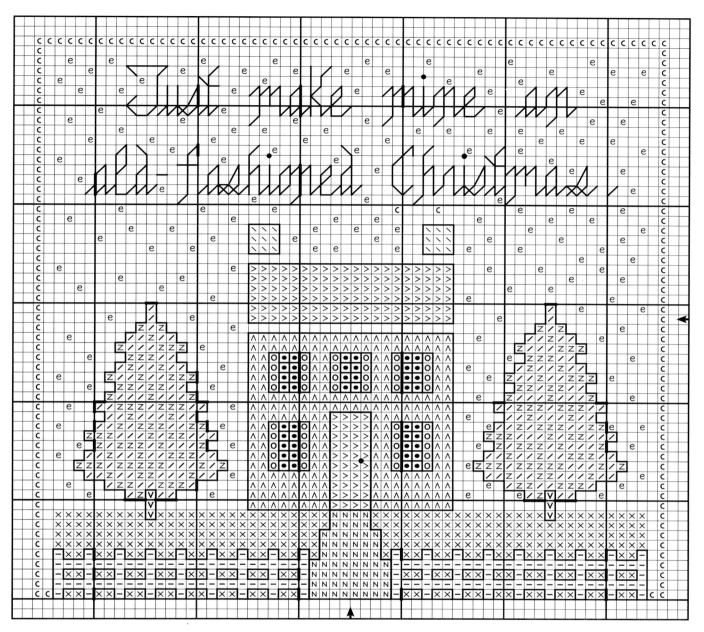

OLD-FASHIONED CHRISTMAS

	DMC	COLOR
-	746	off white
N	3024	brown gray, very light
∧	422	hazelnut brown, light
o	3346	hunter green
>	356	salmon, medium
•	745	yellow, light pale
\	3031	mocha brown, very dark
z	3345	hunter green, dark
/	3347	yellow-green, medium
x [	white	white
	3345	hunter green, dark
e	white	white
∨	420	hazelnut brown, dark
c	793	cornflower blue, medium

Fabric used for model: 14-count ice blue Damask Aida from Wichelt Imports, Inc.
Stitch count: 57H x 62W
Approximate design size:
    14-count—4" x 4 ⅜"
    18-count—3 ¼" x 3 ⅜"

Instructions: Cross stitch using two strands of floss. Backstitch using one strand 3031. Make French knot for door knob using one strand 3031, wrapping around needle twice. When two colors are bracketed together, use one strand of each.

All In A Row

A variety of brightly colored flosses was used to create these holiday-inspired designs. Whether the lucky recipient prefers the stockings in a row hung from a golden garland or the alternating pattern of evergreens and hearts, these designs are sure to brighten each day of her holiday season and lift her spirits every time she reaches for one of these decorated hand towels.

STOCKINGS IN A ROW

	DMC	COLOR
o	742	tangerine, light
V	321	Christmas red
L	603	cranberry
⁄	910	emerald green, dark
c	703	chartreuse

Fabric used for model: 11-count white with green trim Waffle Towel from Norden Crafts

Stitch count: 17H x width of towel

Approximate design size:

11-count—1 ½" x width of towel

Instructions: Cross stitch using three strands of floss. Begin stitching in center of towel and repeat design in each direction to edge of towel.

TREES IN A ROW

	DMC	COLOR
x	321	Christmas red
L	603	cranberry
c	910	emerald green, dark
V	703	chartreuse

Fabric used for model: 11-count white with red trim Waffle Towel from Norden Crafts

Stitch count: 17H x width of towel

Approximate design size:

11-count—2 ¼" x width of towel

Instructions: Cross stitch using three strands of floss. Begin stitching in center of towel and repeat design in each direction to edge of towel.

Joyeux Noël

The holiday season brings with it a wealth of decorating opportunities, and we have found that handmade decorations are always appreciated. You can start, or add to, someone's collection of holiday adornments with this seasonal stitchery they're sure to enjoy. Here finished as a wall hanging, this design will also work well framed.

JOYEUX NOËL		Stitch count: 112H x 83W

Approximate design size:
14-count—8" x 6"
18-count—6 ⅛" x 4 ⅝"
25-count—8 ⅞" x 6 ⅝"

	DMC	COLOR
c	986	forest green, very dark
∕	304	Christmas red, medium
x	640	beige-gray, very dark
∩	822	beige-gray, light
⊃	844	beaver gray, ultra dark
\	948	peach flesh, very light
o	353	peach flesh
■	844	beaver gray, ultra dark
•	746	off white

Fabric used for model: 25-count cream Dublin linen from Zweigart®

Instructions: Cross stitch over two threads using two strands of floss. Backstitch using one strand of floss unless indicated otherwise. Turn to page 140 for finishing instructions.

Backstitch (bs) instructions:
304   border (two strands)
844   remainder of backstitching

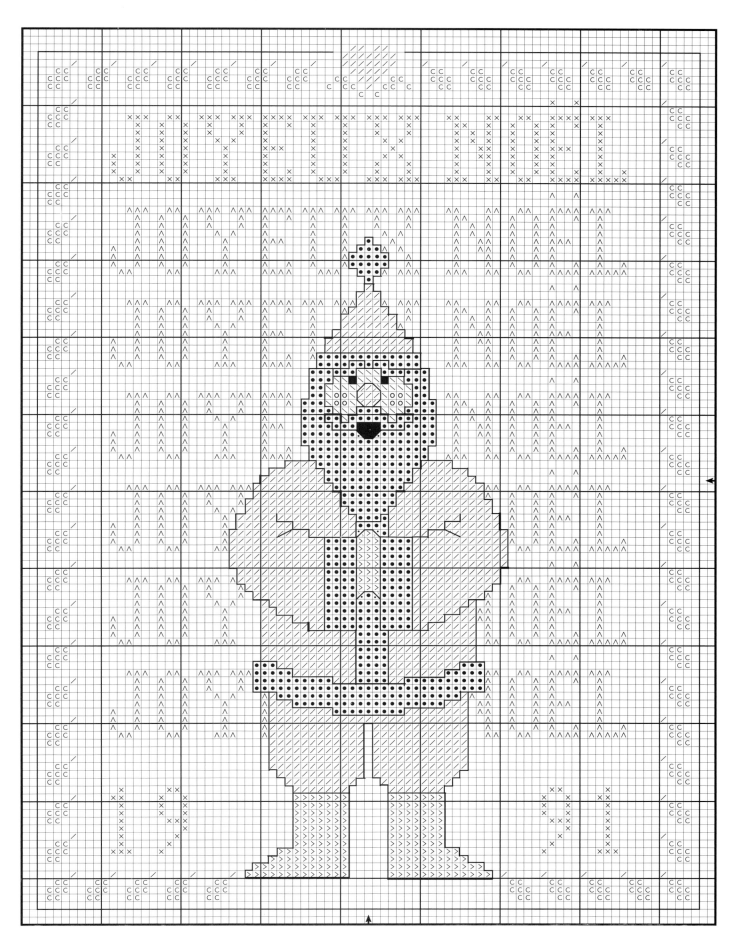

Joyeux Noël Wall Hanging Instructions

Purchase one yard 44/45"-wide fabric that complements the design. From fabric, cut two strips, each 3 ½" x 11", for side borders. Cut two strips, each 3 ½" x 13 ½", for top and bottom borders. Cut three strips, each 6 ½" x 7", for hanging tabs. Cut 13 ½" x 16" piece for backing.

To mark placement for border strips: On right side of design piece, measure 1" outside all edges of stitched design and mark. Following grain of fabric to achieve straight lines, extend marked lines to form a perimeter 1" larger than design on all sides. Mark center of each side of perimeter. Mark center of one long edge of each border strip.

To attach side border strips: With right sides of fabric together and center marks matching, position one border strip so that outside long edge of strip aligns with marked line on one side of design piece. Using a ½" seam allowance, stitch long edge of strip adjacent to marked line. Repeat for other side border strip on other side of design piece. Press so that **wrong** side of border strips face **right** side of design piece.

To attach top and bottom border strips: With right sides of fabric together and center marks matching, position top border strip so that outside long edge of strip aligns with marked line on top of design piece. Using a ½" seam allowance, stitch long edge of strip adjacent to marked line. Repeat for bottom border strip. Press as for side borders.

To make hanging tabs: With right sides of fabric together, fold one strip in half widthwise, aligning 6 ½" raw edges. Using a ½" seam allowance, stitch along raw edges opposite fold to form a tube. Turn right side out and press. Fold tube in half, aligning raw edges, and stitch close to raw edges to form hanging tab. Repeat for remaining tabs.

To join front of wall hanging (design piece with borders) to backing: Beginning at left corner on right side of front, position hanging tabs 1 ⅞" apart along top edge, with raw edges aligned and folded ends of tabs toward stitched design; pin tabs in place. With right sides of fabric together and using a ½" seam allowance, stitch front to backing along side and top edges, catching tabs in seam and leaving bottom edge open for turning. Clip corners, trim seams, and turn right side out. Fold raw edges ½" to inside of wall hanging and slip stitch bottom closed.

General Finishing Instructions

Complete all stitching, following instructions given, before beginning finishing work.

Pillows

To finish a stitched piece as a pillow, determine desired finished size, and cut backing fabric and design to size, allowing for a ½" seam. Place stitched front and backing pieces with right sides together. Stitch around edges, using a ½" seam allowance, and leaving an opening for turning. Trim seams and turn right side out. Stuff to desired fullness and whipstitch opening closed.

When ruffles and/or cording are to be used, the perimeter of the pillow must first be marked on stitched front. Attach ruffles or cording following marking for perimeter, placing right sides of stitched front and ruffle or cording together, making sure that the raw edges of the ruffles or cording and the raw edges of the pillow front are together. (Raw edges must be aligned for decorative trim to be on outside of finished pillow.)

Fringed Coasters And Other Fringed Pieces

To finish a stitched piece as a fringed coaster, cut backing fabric the same size as the stitched front piece. With wrong sides together and a thin layer of polyester filling (cut to fit just inside perimeter of design) centered between layers, machine-stitch around perimeter of design. Fringe front and back of ornament by pulling threads from fabric edges up to machine stitching. To fringe place mats, napkins, and other assorted pieces, omit backing and polyester filling. Machine-stitch around perimeter of piece, stitching equal distances from edge of design on all sides. Pull threads from fabric edges up to machine stitching.

Sachet Bags

To finish a cross stitched piece as a sachet bag, determine desired finished size. Cut design piece to size, adding a ½" seam allowance and cutting the same distance from stitched design on all sides. Cut backing fabric to size. With right sides together and using a ½" seam allowance, stitch front to backing along side and bottom edges, leaving top edge open for turning. Clip corners, trim seams, and turn right side out. Press. Turn raw edges under and press. Stitch lace or other decorative trim around top edge of bag. Fill as desired.

Designs Used With Jar Lids

To use a stitched piece as a decorative addition to a two-piece canning jar lid, center the design over a flat lid and snap the covered flat lid into the ring. Lace the cloth ends together on the back side, trimming if necessary. If jar will be filled with jams, jellies, or other liquids, snap a second flat lid into place, with the laced fabric between the two flat lids. Tie a colorful ribbon around the ring for a special finishing touch.

If you want the cross stitched design to "puff" atop the lid, place a few cotton balls or a small amount of polyester filling between the stitched piece and the first flat lid.

If you wish to trim a jar lid with ruffles around the edge of the ring, place ring on wrong side of stitched piece, centering it over the stitched design. With a disappearing-ink marking pen, draw a circle around the outside perimeter of the ring. Add approximately ¾" seam allowance around drawn circle and cut out shape. Zigzag raw edges to prevent fraying and stitch ruffled lace or other decorative trim close to edge of fabric. To finish, center design over flat lid and snap lid into place in ring.

Hoop Wall Decorations

To finish a stitched piece in a hoop as a wall decoration, follow the general instructions given in "Designs Used With Jar Lids", using hoops instead of jar lids.

Designs With Metal Cans

To finish a design as a decorative covering for a metal can, allow extra fabric on the sides when stitching. Wrap the finished design around a can and whipstitch the free ends together. At bottom of can, fold excess fabric underneath can and whipstitch free ends together. At top of can, fold raw edges to inside of can. Trim with decorative ribbon as desired.

General Instructions For Cross Stitch

Basic Supplies: Even-weave fabric, tapestry needle(s), six-strand embroidery floss, embroidery scissors.

Fabric Preparation: The instructions and yardage for finishing materials have been written and calculated for each of the projects shown stitched on the fabric listed in its color code. Alternate fabric choices have also been listed. If you wish to stitch a design on an alternate fabric, or alter its placement, you will need to re-calculate the finished size of the project, as well as the yardage of finishing materials needed, and make the necessary dimension adjustments when finishing.

Determine size of fabric needed for a project by dividing number of horizontal stitches by thread count of fabric. For example, if a design 35 stitches wide is worked on 14-count fabric, it will cover 2½" (35 divided by 14 equals 2½"). Repeat process for vertical count. Add three inches to all sides of design area, to find dimensions for cutting fabric. Whipstitch edges to prevent fraying.

Floss Preparation: Cut floss into 14" to 18" lengths. Separate all six strands. Reunite number of strands needed and thread needle, leaving one floss end longer than the other.

Where To Start: Start wherever you like! Some designers suggest finding center of fabric and starting there. Others recommend beginning with a central motif, while still others work borders first. Many find fabric center,

count up and back to the left, and start with the uppermost left stitch. Wherever you begin, be sure to leave allowance for all horizontal and vertical stitches so that a 3" fabric margin is left around perimeter of design.

Should you choose to begin at the center point, find it by folding fabric from top to bottom and then from left to right. Use a straight pin to mark upper left corner at junction of folds, then unfold fabric. Pin will be in center of fabric.

After deciding where to begin on fabric, find same point on graph. Each square on graph represents one stitch. Those squares containing a symbol (i.e., X, T, O) indicate that a stitch should be made in that space over those threads. Different symbols represent different colors of floss for stitches. (See color code of chart.) They may also indicate partial or decorative stitches. Familiarize yourself with color code before you begin stitching. Even-weave fabric may be stretched over an embroidery hoop to facilitate stitching.

Stitching The Design: Using the illustrations on page 142, stitch design, completing all full and partial cross stitches first. Cross all full cross stitches in same direction to achieve a smooth surface appearance. Work backstitches second, and any decorative stitches last.

Helpful Hints For Stitching: *Do not knot floss.* Instead, catch end on back of work with first few stitches. As you stitch, pull floss through fabric "holes" with one stroke, not several short ones. The moment you feel resistance from floss, cease pulling. Consistent tension on floss results in a smoother look for stitches. Drop your needle frequently to allow floss to untwist. It twists naturally as you stitch, and as it gets shorter it must be allowed to untwist more often. To begin a new color on project, prepare floss and secure new strands as noted. To end stitching, run floss under completed stitches and clip remaining strands close to surface. Many times it is necessary to skip a few spaces (threads) on the fabric in order to continue a row of stitches in the same color. If you must skip an area covering more than ¼", end stitching as described above and begin again at next point. This procedure prevents uneven tension on the embroidery surface, and snagging on back. It also keeps colors from showing through unstitched areas. Do not carry thread over an area that will remain unstitched.

When You Are Finished: For designs using cotton or linen floss on cotton or linen even-weave fabric, hand wash piece with mild detergent in warm water. Rinse thoroughly with cold water, roll in terry towel, and squeeze gently to remove excess moisture. *Do not wring.* Unroll towel and allow piece to dry until barely damp. Iron on padded surface with design face down, using iron's medium setting for heat. A press cloth is seldom necessary, but will help prevent shine on dark fabrics. **Note:** Acrylics, acrylic blends, wools or silks must be treated differently when cleaning. Check manufacturer's guidelines for special cleaning instructions.

Basic stitches over 1 thread

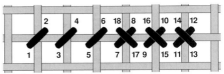
Basic cross stitch

Basic half cross stitch

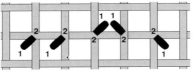
Basic quarter stitch

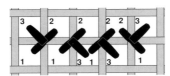
Three-quarter stitches—various positions

Two three-quarter stitches in one square, using two different floss colors

Basic stitches over 2 threads

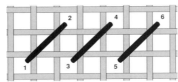
Half cross stitch

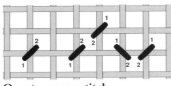
Quarter cross stitch

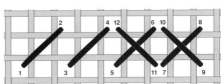
Full cross stitch

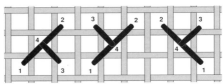
Three-quarter cross stitch

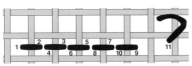
Basic backstitch

Backstitch—showing variations

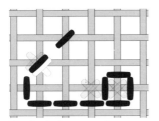
Backstitch across two three-quarter stitches and around full cross

Shoppers' Guide

Four Seasons
Wooden Basket: From The Garden Shop, Birmingham, Alabama
Pitcher: *Fruit* by Stangl, Trenton, New Jersey
Plate: From a private collection
Fabrics: Wall Hanging: 28-count tan Jobelan from Wichelt Imports, Inc.; Jar Lids: 14-count white Aida; Place Mat and Napkin (used as table runner and bread cover): 14-count country oatmeal Royal Classics from Charles Craft, Inc.

Vegetable Squares
Delft Tiles: From a private collection
Hand-painted Mold: From a private collection
Fabric: 14-count white Aida

Flower Basket
Mirrored Tray: From a private collection
Soaps: From Bath Express, Birmingham, Alabama
Nail Brush: From Pier 1 Imports
Antique Card: Purchased at a flea market
Flowered Dish: *Moss Rose* by Royal Albert
Fabrics: 14-count white KitchenMates towel, and 14-count buttered almond KitchenMates towel from Charles Craft, Inc.

Greetings!
Oak Towel Bar: From Wheatland Crafts, Inc.
Fringed towel: From a private collection
Copper Tea Kettle: From a private collection
Fabrics: 14-count ivory Aida; Joan Kessler for Concord Fabrics, Inc.

Welcome To Our Home
Curtains: Purchased at a local fabric store
Fabric: 27-count natural brown linen from Norden Crafts

Autumn Welcome
Fabric: 25-count Floba® from Zweigart®

Give Thanks
Creamer: From a private collection
Cups and Saucers: From a private collection
Pewter Candlestick: From a private collection
Fabric: 25-count cream Dublin linen from Zweigart®

My Quilt And I
Quilts: From a private collection
Cat: From a private collection
Fabric: 27-count cream linen from Norden Crafts

Don't Forget
Cross Stitch Black Board/Bulletin Board: From Wheatland Crafts, Inc.
Fabrics: College: 14-count antique white Aida from Charles Craft, Inc.; Kitchen: 14-count cream Aida; Child: 25-count cream Lugana® from Zweigart®

Spring Blossom Trio
Wooden Bunny: From a private collection
Wooden Easel: From David's Arts and Frames, Birmingham, Alabama
Wooden Box: From Wheatland Crafts, Inc.
Fabrics: Floral Bouquet: 12-count blue and white Arno from Wichelt Imports, Inc.; Tulip Basket: 14-count ivory Aida; Hydrangea: 18-count white Aida

Floral Heart
Heart-shaped Footstool: From Wheatland Crafts, Inc.
Cup and Saucer: From a private collection
Book: From Dorothy McDaniels Florist, Birmingham, Alabama
Fabric: 32-count cream Belfast linen from Zweigart®

Flower Repeat
Fabrics: 14-count white Aida, 8-count white Aida, and 11-count white Aida; Pink floral chintz by Laura Ashley
Lace: Purchased at a local fabric store

Girl With Umbrella
Fabric: 22-count Dresden blue Oslo from Zweigart®

Weather Vane
Tea Strainer and Teapot: From a private collection
Quilt Square: From House Of Quilts, Springville, Alabama
Fabrics: 25-count Floba® from Zweigart®; Pansy by Laura Ashley

Hearts In The Round
Wooden Box: From Sudberry House
Cup and Saucer: From a private collection
Fabric: 14-count white Aida

Autumn's Gift
Fabric: 18-count ecru pre-finished Continental Collection bookmark from Craft World®, Inc.

When This I See
Fabric: 29-count natural Glenshee linen from Anne Powell, Ltd.

ABC
Fabric: 14-count ivory Aida on apron from Lollipop Designs

Tin Can Treasures
Fabrics: Lollipop Shop: 14-count white Aida; Late To School: 18-count ivory Aida

Mirror Image
Pitcher: From a private collection
Cathedral Mirror: From Wheatland Crafts, Inc.
Fabric: 14-count white Aida

Lunchtime Pals
Silverware: From Kmart, Birmingham, Alabama
Fabric: 14-count white quilted bibs with trim (green, red, pink, and blue) from The Janlynn Corporation

Skipping Rope
Wooden Box: From Anne Brinkley Design Co.
Fabric: 18-count white Aida

Geometric Pincushion
Cup and Saucer: From a private collection
Needlecase and Thimble: From a private collection
Locket: From a private collection
Fabric: 18-count white Aida

Sit With Me
Cup and Saucer: From a private collection
Glass tray: From a private collection
Fabric: 14-count ivory Aida

Trusted Friend Sampler
Plate: Purchased at a flea market
Scissors: From Qualität, made in Germany
Fabric: 26-count golden flax linen from Wichelt Imports, Inc.

The World's Best
Fabric: 14-count antique white Aida from Charles Craft, Inc.

Posey Alphabet
Scissors and Thimble: From Qualität, made in Germany
Fabrics: 14-count cream small, medium, and large scissor cases; 14-count white Aida tissue holder; and 27-count off white sachet bag from The Janlynn Corporation; 14-count ecru/weathered tan twill Borderlines Fingertips™ towel from Charles Craft, Inc.; 18-count cream pre-finished Continental Collection bookmark from Craft World®, Inc.

Miles Apart-Close At Heart
Rabbit Figurine: From a private collection

Linen: Purchased at a local antique store
Fabric: 27-count cream linen from Norden Crafts

Two For Tea
Cup and Saucer: From a private collection
Fabrics: 27-count ivory linen from Norden Crafts; *Sweetwater* by Waverly; Pink floral with stripe by Laura Ashley

A Friend
Plate: Haviland & Co., Limoges, France
Fabric: 14-count antique white Aida from Charles Craft, Inc.

Blessed Are The Piece-makers
Fabric: 14-count cream Aida

He Who Indulges Bulges
Acrylic Magnet: From Wheatland Crafts, Inc.
Fabric: 14-count white Aida

Welcome Little One
Wooden Sheep: From a private collection
Wooden Heart Shelf: From a private collection
Wooden Candlesticks: From a private collection
Fabrics: 14-count forget-me-not blue Aida from Wichelt Imports, Inc.; yellow bib from Charles Craft, Inc.

Mother's Day
Fabric: 18-count ivory Aida

Baby Things
Fabrics: Animal Fair, Four Lambs, and Boy's Toys: 14-count white Aida bottle warmer from The Janlynn Corporation; 14-count white Park Avenue Fingertips™ towel from Charles Craft, Inc.

Treat Bags
Fabric: 14-count white Aida
Ribbon: Purchased at a local variety store

Woven Ribbon And Sweet Sixteen
Porcelain Trinket Boxes: From Anne Brinkley Design Co.
Plate: From a private collection
Fabrics: 18-count white Aida; Pink Floral Chintz by Laura Ashley

Happy Birthday!
Fabric: 27-count white Super Linen from Charles Craft, Inc.

Celebrate In Style
Crystal, Silver, and Cranberry Glassware: From a private collection

Fabrics: 27-count white Super Linen from Charles Craft, Inc.; Rose Chintz by Laura Ashley

Thee I Love
Silver and China: From a private collection
Fabric: 25-count moss green Lugana® from Zweigart®

Father's Day Duo
Fabric: 14-count Fiddler's Lite from Charles Craft, Inc.

For Graduation Day
Fabric: 14-count white Aida

Happy Hanukkah
Fabric: 28-count ivory linen from Wichelt Imports, Inc.

Celebrate Retirement!
Golfer's Mug: From the Russ Berrie Company Catalog, Oakland, New Jersey
Fabric: 14-count white Aida

Christmas Village
Plate: *Blue Spongeware*
Coffee Mug And Fork: Purchased at a local antique store
Fabrics: 14-count colonial blue place mat, and 14-count white place mat from Craft World®, Inc.

Peace On Earth Sampler
Wooden Frame: Purchased at a local craft store
Pitcher, Lamp, and Photo Frame: From a private collection
Fabrics: 14-count summer khaki Aida, and 14-count cream Aida

Merry Christmas
Cloth Bunny: From a private collection
Antique Oil Lamp: Purchased at a local antique store
Fabric: 32-count white Belfast linen from Zweigart®

Holiday Lights
Stainless: *Elegance*
Fabric: 18-count white Aida on red/white place mat from Tish & Amy Originals

Christmas Animal Wreath
Teddy Bear Garland: From Michael's, Inc., Birmingham, Alabama
Fabric: 14-count white Aida

First Christmas
Wooden Frames: From David's Arts and

Frames, Birmingham, Alabama
Teddy Bear: From a private collection
Wooden Beads: From The Christmas Cottage, Birmingham, Alabama
Striped Tins: From Hickory Farms of Ohio
Fabric: 27-count white linen from Wichelt Imports, Inc.

Holly Motif
Fabric: 14-count white Park Avenue Fingertips™ towel from Charles Craft, Inc.

Gifts To Share
Fabric: 14-count white Aida

Christmas And Welcome Coasters
Coffee Mugs: From Barnie's Coffee And Tea Company, Birmingham, Alabama
Plate: From Pier 1 Imports
Fabrics: Christmas: 27-count natural brown and cream linen from Norden Crafts; Welcome: 27-count natural brown linen from Norden Crafts

Noel
Wooden Frame and Easel: From David's Arts and Frames, Birmingham, Alabama
Fabric: 27-count natural Super Linen from Charles Craft, Inc.

Just Make Mine An Old-Fashioned Christmas
Wooden Houses: From a private collection
Fabric: 14-count ice blue Damask Aida from Wichelt Imports, Inc.

Joyeux Noël
Antique Sewing Machine and Tools: From a private collection
Wooden Candle Holder: From a private collection
Fabric: 25-count cream Dublin linen from Zweigart®

All In A Row
Soap: From Crabtree & Evelyn
Sponge: From Pier 1 Imports
Dish: Olde Alton Ware, England
Fabrics: 11-count white with green trim and 11-count white with red trim Waffle Towels from Norden Crafts

Items not listed in "Shoppers' Guide" are either commonly available, antiques, or are from private collections.

Special thanks to Mrs. E. P. Beaumont, Mr. and Mrs. Jerome Billings, Mr. and Mrs. W. H. MacMillan, and Mrs. Glenda Parker, Birmingham, Alabama, for providing the photography locations in this book.